Traditional Mexican Style Exteriors

Text by Donna McMenamin

Photography by Richard Loper

Schiffer Publishing Ltd

4880 Lower Valley Road, Atglen, PA 19310 USA

Dedication

To all the *maestros* who pour their hearts
and souls into creating the architectural
details and works of art that beautify our
homes, and to the laborers who install them.

Library of Congress Cataloging-in-Publication Data

McMenamin, Donna
 Traditional Mexican style exteriors / text by Donna
McMenamin; photography by Richard Loper.
 p. cm.
 ISBN 0-7643-1726-1 (hardcover)
1. Architecture--United States--Details. 2. Architecture--Mexico-
-details. 3. Architecture--United States--Mexican influences.
4. Decoration and ornament, Architectural--United States.
5. Decoration and ornament, Architectural--Mexico. 6. Architecture, Domestic--United States. 7. Architecture, Domestic-
-Mexico. I. Title.
NA2840 .M38 2003
728'.0972--dc21
                    2002013515

Text Copyright © 2003 by Donna McMenamin
Photographs Copyright © 2003 by Richard Loper

Designed by "Sue"
Type set in Impact/Korinna BT

ISBN: 0-7643-1726-1
Printed in China

Title page: In this intimate patio, a large mesquite tree grows in front
of a recessed *cantera* stone fountain in the stone wall. An unusual
flooring of bricks compose a sunburst pattern, and sword ferns and
bamboo add to the tropical atmosphere. *Casa Heyne.*

Published by Schiffer Publishing Ltd.
4880 Lower Valley Road
Atglen, PA 19310
Phone: (610) 593-1777; Fax: (610) 593-2002
E-mail: Info@schifferbooks.com
Please visit our web site catalog at
www.schifferbooks.com

This book may be purchased from the publisher.
Include $3.95 for shipping. Please try your bookstore
first.
We are always looking for people to write books on
new and related subjects. If you have an idea for a
book please contact us at the above address.
You may write for a free catalog.

In Europe, Schiffer books are distributed by
Bushwood Books
6 Marksbury Avenue
Kew Gardens
Surrey TW9 4JF England
Phone: 44 (0) 20-8392-8585; Fax: 44 (0) 20-8392-9876
E-mail: info@bushwoodbooks.co.uk
Free postage in the UK. Europe: air mail at cost.
Please try your bookstore first.

Acknowledgements

A book such as this does not happen without a great deal of cooperation from old friends and acquaintances, and of course new *amigos* we made along the way. We would like to take this opportunity to thank them all. First and foremost, we wholeheartedly express our gratitude to all of the homeowners who relinquished their privacy and graciously gave us access to their personal domains. Not only did they graciously open their doors, but many had to do so in the early morning hours. (While a 6:30 am schedule might not seem too early for many of us in the States, for Mexico, it is unheard of.) Many of the homeowners fed us along the way and provided transportation, which made lugging our equipment much easier, and for that we are extremely appreciative. Our warmest thanks go to John & Nancy Alegret, Stan Avison & Bruce Ericksen, Craig Baugh, Thomas E. Black III, Tonia & Bob Clark, Carol & Roger Collier, Sande Deitch, Anna Franklin, Rhea & Leon Gary and their agent Mary Barbara Scott, Marc Gerson, Milagros & Rafael Ghinis, Ricardo González and Maria Ramírez, Nicholas Power & Penelope Haskew, Luis Felix Hernández & Dorothy Mann de Hernández, Janet & Fred Heyne and their staff, with a special thanks to Raul Briones, Rachel Horn, Richard Leet and his staff, Bill & Heidi LeVasseur and staff, John & Bettie Moser, Jorge & Maria Peña, Mary Ann & Ron Peterson, Sue Pittman and her staff, Bill Reiner & Stanton Gray, Terry & Jack Reinhart, Judith Richardson, Judith Roberts, Raye & Noble Robinson, Isidra Salazar Olmos, Dean & Filomena Saxton, Lynn & Dave Shaw, and Mike & Jayne Wachs. Additionally, there are those who wished to remain anonymous, and as much as we would like to acknowledge them here, we must respect their wishes, but a big thanks to them as well.

In San Miguel de Allende, we owe a huge thank you to Jennifer Hamilton, who single-handedly sought out some of the finest San Miguel *casas* for us to scout. She supplied us with an extraordinary amount of information regarding some sixty homes in San Miguel prior to our arrival and she continued her support throughout the entire trip. We could not have accomplished the San Miguel shoot without her, and we are absolutely indebted to her. *Muchas gracias*, Jennifer.

Several others gave their time, assistance, and encouragement along the way, including Suzy and Roberto Alvarado, Patti Behr, Dave Carter, Lou Christine, Nancy Dusseau, Clyde Ellis, Christopher & Caroline Fallon, Bonnie Gibson, Bob & Jennifer Haas, Alice Dale Kimsey, Barbara Kraus, Bonnie Kuykendall, Christy Martin, Jim Miegs, Barbara & Jeffrey Minker, Mary Mohr, Salvador Orozco, Jed Paradies, Debra Raeber, Rick & Marybeth Rosenthal, Ron Slaughter, Linda Solomon, Joel Stocker & Tom Brightman, Nancy Swickard, and Sondra Zell.

Gracias to Joe Ingegneri, Tim Bosveld, and Jose Enriquez of Dunn-Edwards Corporation for supplying specific paint color sample cards.

Religious art experts and dealers, James Caswell (Santa Monica) and Martha Egan (Santa Fe), were consulted to identify *Santos* and *retablos*. In addition, when stumped as to the exact origin of an old California tile mural at Red Thunder Ranch, antique tile dealer, Scott Wells (Los Angeles) came to the rescue. We are grateful for knowledgeable friends.

We were both extremely pleased that architect Rafael Rios-Ghinis agreed to be interviewed, and provided explanations for those illusive architectural terms, like *ojo de buey*. As an architect from Mexico, now designing and residing in Tucson, his insights proved invaluable in understanding the Mexican home from both sides of the border.

Frank Stryker and Sparky Heinig identified most of the plants in these photos and graciously consented to an interview for a discussion of landscaping in desert climates. We hope that you will find it helpful in your own landscaping considerations.

Kudos to our editor and publisher, Nancy and Peter Schiffer, who never hesitated when approached about the concept of this book and have been supportive as always.

We should not forget that the beauty of these homes and their lush surroundings is founded upon the dreams and visions of architects and designers. Without this starting point, their drawing boards, none of these homes would have become a reality. These homes are works of art and will remain standing long after our time has passed.

And finally, a very special and affectionate thank-you to our spouses, David and Linda, who endured our absences from home and gave us the time and space necessary to complete this project.

Credits

Name of home: **Allison/Henry Trost House**
Year Built: 1902
Owners: Dean and Filomena Saxton
City: Tucson, Arizona
Architect: Henry Trost
Landscape: Dean Saxton
Pages: 41, 71

Name of home: **La Casa que Abraza el Cielo** (The House that Embraces the Sky)
Year Built: 1998
Owner: Anonymous
City: Tucson, Arizona
Architect: Ron Robinette
Landscape: Richard Wogisch
Interior Decorator: Christy Martin of Studio Encanto
Builder: Mike Wachs of Mike Wachs Construction Company
Pages: 50, 75, 80, 107, 108, 114, 116, 124, 143, 176, 177

Name of home: **Casa de Alegret**
Year Built: 1986—additions 1999
Owners: John and Nancy Alegret
City: Tucson, Arizona
Architects: David Goff (original home) David Wilson (additions)
Pages: 45, 58, 59, 62, 73, 105, 128, 129, 152, 154, 182, 183

Caption Designation: **Casa de Black**
Owner: Thomas E. Black III
City: Tucson, Arizona
Landscape: Plants of Distinction
Pages: 86, 136, 142, 144, 149, 184-187

Name of home: **Casa Chorro**
Year built: circa 1800, remodeled 1999
Owner: Richard Leet
City: San Miguel de Allende, Guanajuato, Mexico
Pages: 32, 33, 62, 104, 105, 134, 168, 169

Caption Designation: **Casa de Clark**
Year Built: 1997
Owners: Tonia and Bob Clark
City: Houston, Texas
Architect: Michael T. Landrum
Landscape Architect: Sarah W. Lake
Page: 175

Name of home: **Casa de la Condessa** (House of the Contessa)
Year built: circa 1960, remodeled 2000
Owner: Sande Deitch
City: San Miguel de Allende, Guanajuato, Mexico
Architectural Designers: Caroline and Christopher Fallon (remodeling)
Landscape Designer: Alfonso Alarcón
Interior Decorator: Sande Deitch and Christopher Fallon
Pages: 36-38, 68, 79, 82-85, 115, 116, 122, 130, 167

Name of home: **Casa de la Cuesta** (House on the Hill) (Bed & Breakfast)
Year built: 1999
Owners: Bill and Heidi LeVasseur
City: San Miguel de Allende, Guanajuato, Mexico
Arquitecto: Francisco Molina
Pages: 18, 19, 63, 91, 113, 127, 145, 176

Caption Designation: **Casa de Franklin**
Owner: Anna Franklin
City: Tucson, Arizona
Pages: 56, 57, 141, 147, 171, 172

Caption Designation: **Casa de Ghinis**
Owners: Milagros and Rafael R. Ghinis
Year Built: 1930, addition: 1995
Arquitecto: Rafael-Rios Ghinis (addition)
City: Tucson, Arizona
Pages: 39, 60, 66, 71, 138, 148, 153, 155, 157, 158

Caption Designation: **Casa de Hernández**
Year Built: 1972
Owners: Luis Félix Hernández y Dorothy Mann de Hernández
City: San Miguel de Allende, Guanajuato, Mexico
Page: 23

Name of home: **Casa Heyne**
Year Built: 2000
Owners: Janet and Fred Heyne
City: San Miguel de Allende, Guanajuato, Mexico
Arquitecto: Pedro Urquiza
Landscape Designer: Timeteo Wachter
Pages: Title page, 42-44, 61, 64, 67, 69, 109, 110, 112, 135, 160, 162, 163

Name of home: **Casa Kino**
Year Built: 1998
Owner: Marc Gerson
City: Tucson, Arizona
Architect: John Gabb and Marc Gerson, Architectural Designer
Landscape: Marc Gerson and Plants of Distinction
Interior Decorator: Marc Gerson of Marc New West Design, Inc.
Pages: 51, 52, 71, 72, 98, 131, 147, 150, 151, 154, 158, 171

Name of home: **La Casa Lomita Linda** (The Pretty Little Hill House)
Year Built: 1985, remodeled 2000
Owners: Roger and Carol Collier
City: Tucson, Arizona
Architect: David Shambach and James Meigs, architectural designer (remodeling)
Landscape: Dan Elder
Interior Decorator: Diane Love
Pages: 46, 47, 74, 81, 86, 87, 128, 132, 133, 137, 148, 152, 153, 156, 157, 178

Caption Designation: **Casa de Moser**
Owners: John and Bettie Moser
Year Built: 1990
City: Tucson, Arizona
Architectural Designer: Mike and Jayne Wachs of Mike Wachs Construction Company
Pages: 30, 31, 59, 76, 106, 117-119, 131, 146, 170

Name of home: **Casa del Parque** (House in the Park)
Year built: 1995
Owners: Ricardo González and Maria Ramírez
City: San Miguel de Allende, Guanajuato, Mexico
Arquitecto: Manuel Barbosa
Landscape: José Bautista
Pages: 18, 102, 175

Name of home: **Casa de los Perros** (House of the Dogs)
Year built: unknown, remodeled 2001
Owner: Sue R. Pittman
City: San Miguel de Allende, Guanajuato, Mexico
Architectural Designer: Christopher Fallon (remodeling)
Interior Decorator: Sue R. Pittman
Pages: 54, 65, 102, 127, 140, 141, 144, 161

Name of home: **Casa Poco a Poco** (House Little by Little)
Year built: 1991
Owners: Jorge and Maria Eugenia Peña
City: San Miguel de Allende, Guanajuato, Mexico
Page: 170

Caption Designation: **Casa de Reiner y Gray**
Year Built: 2000
Owners: Bill Reiner and Stanton Gray
City: San Miguel de Allende, Guanajuato, Mexico
Arquitecto: Luis Camarena
Landscape Designer: Tim Wachter
Pages: 52, 53, 173, 174

Caption Designation: **Casa de Reinhart**
Year built: circa 1960, remodeled 1995
Owners: Jack Reinhart and Therese Kutt Reinhart
City: San Miguel de Allende, Guanajuato, Mexico
Arquitecto: Juan Carlos Valdés A. (remodeling)
Pages: 34, 35, 65, 80, 103, 126, 159, 164-167

Caption Designation: **Casa de Roberts**
Year built: 1970
Owner: Judith Roberts
City: San Miguel de Allende, Guanajuato, Mexico
Architectural Designer: Francisco Garcia Valencia
Pages: 32, 68, 106

Caption Designation: **Casa de Robinson**
Owners: Raye and Noble Robinson
Year Built: 1999
City: Tucson, Arizona
Architect: Matthew Hamilton
Builder: Michael Nicholas
Landscape: Harlows
Interior Decorator: Owner, Virginia Manzer, and Sharmin Pool-Bok
Pages: 47, 66, 70, 125

Caption Designation: **Casa de Salazar Olmos**
Year Built: 1995
Owners: Isidra Salazar Olmos
City: Santa Rosa de Linda, Guanajuato, Mexico
Page: 111

Name of home: **Casa del Sol y Luna** (House of the Sun & Moon)
Year Built: 2000
Owners: Donna and David McMenamin
City: Tucson, Arizona
Arquitecto: Rafael Rios-Ghinis
Pages: 24, 25, 55, 67, 78, 97, 98, 115, 123, 137, 140, 146, 150, 156, 158, 160, 161

Caption Designation: **Casa de Wachs**
Owners: Michael and Jayne Wachs
Year Built: 1995
City: Tucson, Arizona
Architectural Designer: Mike and Jayne Wachs of Mike Wachs Construction Company
Interior Decorator: Jayne Wachs
Pages: 39, 98, 120, 133, 161

Name of home: **El Castillo** (The Castle)
Year Built: 1932, outdoor *sala* added 1999
Owners: Mary Ann and Ron Peterson
City: Tucson, Arizona
Architect: Josias Joesler (original) and Alexandra Hayes (addition)
Pages: 14-17, 77, 92-95, 122, 135, 179

Name of home: **Estrella de la Mañana** (Morning Star)
Year built: circa 1690s, remodeled 1996 into existing walls
Owners: Rhea and Leon Gary
City: San Miguel de Allende, Guanajuato, Mexico
Architect: Hal Box (remodeling)
Landscape: Joseph Turner
Interior Decorator: Marsha Brown and owner
Pages: 8, 40, 99-101, 113

Name of home: **La Flor del Desierto** (The Flower of the Desert)
Year Built: 1998, guest-house added 2001
Owners: Dave Shaw and Lynn Mitchener Shaw
City: Tucson, Arizona
Architectural Designer: James Meigs
Cantera Master: Don Lupe Garcia
Wood Master: Salvador Orozco
Pages: 48, 49, 59, 69, 76, 88-90, 114, 119, 138, 139, 180

Name of home: **La Haciendita** (The Little Hacienda)
Year Built: unknown—remodeled 1989 into existing walls
Owners: Judith Richardson
City: San Miguel de Allende, Guanajuato, Mexico
Landscape Designer: Guadelupe Rangel
Pages: 26, 170

Name of home: **Red Thunder Ranch**
Year Built: 1922, remodeled 1996
Owners: Stan Avison and Bruce Ericksen
City: Corona de Tucson, Arizona
Architect: Bob Taylor (remodeling)
Pages: 20-23, 96, 97, 121, 135, 180, 181

Name of home: **Villa Scorpio al Puente** (Villa of the Scorpion by the Bridge) (Bed & Breakfast)
Year built: circa 1730s, remodeling on-going
Owners: Nicholas Power and Penelope Haskew
City: San Miguel de Allende, Guanajuato, Mexico
Pages: 26-29, 151

Author's Preface

After the release of *Popular Arts of Mexico 1850-1950*, I was asked the same question over and over—How did you get the idea for the book, get it started, etc.? It appears that readers are quite interested in these facts, so with that in mind, allow me to explain how *Traditional Mexican Style Interiors* and *Traditional Mexican Style Exteriors* came to be.

With construction completed on *Casa del Sol y Luna*, I embarked on another trip to Mexico with my longtime shopping companion, Marilyn, in order to buy appropriate finishing accessories. As our trip was drawing to a close, our friend Jorge, wanted to show us his home and surrounding neighborhood. We only had a few minutes, as we were enroute to the airport, but in that brief period, what I saw made a profound impact on me—the architecture, its details, and the colors of the *casas* were incredibly beautiful! I turned to Marilyn and made the statement "there is a book in here somewhere."

I guess with that small declaration, I planted a seed somewhere in my subconscious because I could not seem to shake the idea, no matter how hard I tried— and I did try. I really did not want to take on the task of another book, especially one where I did not have any sources. At least in *Popular Arts*, I knew where collections resided and those would become that book's foundation, but for this project, I had no starting point. How would I find the homes, and once I did, would I be able to persuade the owners to let me in for a peek? Would they subsequently grant permission for photography? Those details worried me, but I put them aside for the moment.

I presented the book idea to my husband, David. I wanted his opinion on the concept and his reaction to me taking on another project of this magnitude. He thought it was a good idea and I was out of the starting blocks, so to speak, but just ahead of me, several hurdles required clearance.

Richard Loper, the photographer from *Popular Arts*, was the first hurdle—would he be interested in becoming a partner in this endeavor? Fortunately, he was very enthusiastic and agreed to the project without much hesitation. Next up, could I persuade Rafael Rios-Ghinis, a Mexican architect, to agree to an interview and provide technical support as needed? *Si*. Two hurdles safely maneuvered and another one approaching. What would Schiffer Publishing think of the concept and would they agree to publish it? Again, there was enthusiasm. Now, with a willing partner/photographer, a Mexican architect, and a publisher, I was definitely in the race.

Looming down the track were huge hurdles—finding appropriate homes and subsequently gaining access and permissions. I began in my own back yard—Tucson, (a.k.a., the Old Pueblo). The Spanish settled Tucson in 1776 and Mexico controlled the city from 1821 until the Gadsden Purchase of 1854. Four mountain ranges—Santa Catalinas, Santa Ritas, Rincons and the Tucson Mountains—surround this beautiful city that sits in the saguaro-studded Sonoran desert. It is no surprise that the Old Pueblo lends itself to Mexican architecture: (1) the topography is similar to Mexico, (2) there is a long Spanish history, (3) the close proximity to the Mexican border (about sixty miles), and (4) Tucson averages three hundred sixty days of sunshine per year. As with Mexico, outdoor living is a way of life here and the homes are designed to capitalize on that fact along with the incredible mountain and desert vistas. After several months of scouting, the Tucson shoot became a reality and includes homes built as early as 1902 and as late as 2000.

With the Tucson photography completed, it was time to focus on San Miguel de Allende, a city with incredible architecture located one hundred eighty miles northwest of Mexico City, in the state of Guanajuato. Founded in 1542, it is a Spanish Colonial jewel that has become one of Mexico's protected National Monuments. Because of that fact, any new construction in the historic district must conform to the colonial style, complete with a strict set of architectural guidelines. Keeping that in mind, it might prove difficult to ascertain the age of the *casas* presented here, without peeking at the Credits page, as we illustrate homes built from the 18th century to the present.

I chose to organize both of these books by category, as this method has proved itself invaluable to decorators, architects, builders and homeowners. For example, if you are looking for kitchen ideas and inspiration, it is a simple matter to peruse the chapter on *cocinas* in *Traditional Mexican Style Interiors*. In addition, if you want to view one house in its entirety, please refer to the Credits pages of both books.

An important aspect of the Mexican home is color, and I decided early into the project to try to include the name and manufacturer of paint colors we encountered along the way, whenever possible. Unfortunately, this was not feasible for the homes photographed in San Miguel, because, in all cases, the painters mix the colors on-site with several different powdered pigments and a lime-wash known as *cal*. However, with the Tucson homes, we were more fortunate. You will find the paint color name in the caption, and further information in the Paint Sample Illustrations in Appendix 2.

Aside from paint, there is one particular *talavera* tile (*medio-pañuelo*) that we found installed quite frequently in these homes. It is one of the most versatile tile designs ever produced, due to its color variety and installation patterns. Therefore, I felt it might be beneficial to provide an illustration as further clarification (see Appendix 1).

I believe that you will discover that traditional Mexican homes are some of the most beautiful, warm and inviting homes ever designed. Nothing can quite compare with their architectural lines and details, gardens, *portales,* and COLORS! At times, they may require some remodeling to enlarge or add rooms, a new coat of paint, and other maintenance issues, but if elevations and interiors are designed traditionally, they should warrant no other updating. In contrast, I remember my 1970's contemporary style home with its chocolate brown shag carpeting, painted kitchen cabinetry (lime green and lemon yellow) and green laminated countertops. I also remember a few years later when all of that was out of style. Traditional Mexican homes are design classics and their timeless beauty never goes out of vogue.

A final note: Even though many hurdles were cleared to complete this project, I will never be a track star. One hour after photographing the final home in San Miguel (the final hurdle), I stumbled and fell, which resulted in a broken foot and an added bonus of torn ligaments. Being bed-ridden for several weeks did have its benefits though—I directed my full attention to writing, and therefore both books were ahead of schedule by several months. This was not an easy race to run, but I believe that *Traditional Mexican Style Interiors* and *Traditional Mexican Style Exteriors* are worthy of the effort spent.

Photographer's Preface

Growing up in Wilmington, Delaware, blessed with parents who continually stood by me, allowed me to reach for my dreams. Fond memories of my childhood include my father's basement where he built me a photographic darkroom so that I could explore my newfound hobby. It was also in this dusty environment where my second passion developed. I remember searching through my dad's scrap bin to find two pieces of wood that when put together would form some utilitarian function. Both of these hobbies illustrated my desire for creative expression and two interesting careers were born from that Delaware basement.

In 1995, Donna McMenamin approached me with an unusual project. She was working on a book and needed approximately three hundred Mexican art objects photographed, in six different cities and had allotted ten days for the shoot. Needless to say, the thought of actually accomplishing this feat seemed difficult—if not impossible! However, I accepted the challenge and for the next week and a half, I was exposed to a new world that I never knew existed. I fell in love with straw mosaics and the graphics of Tlaquepaque style pottery and knew in an instant that I wanted to collect these two Mexican art forms.

It was not until my work began on *Traditional Mexican Style: Interiors* and *Traditional Mexican Style: Exteriors* that I truly gained an appreciation for the art objects that I had photographed in *Popular Arts*. With San Miguel being home to many outstanding artists and craftsmen, opportunities arose that afforded us close-up observations of works in progress. Just watching the *maestros* carving *cantera* stone and wood, hammering copper, painting pottery/tiles, and punching tin was an unexpected and added bonus. My appreciation for their workmanship grew as I photographed *talavera*-tiled kitchens and bathrooms, carved doors, *cantera,* tinwork, and all of the various art objects installed and displayed in homes throughout these two books.

Being a self-taught furniture maker, I know firsthand what it takes to master a craft and everywhere I looked in these homes, I could see the various artisans' hands at work. In the United States, we are accustomed to construction styles that are somewhat sterile, square, and plumb and we did not witness much of this in Mexico. Not to say everything is off-kilter—on the contrary! Most everything we saw had curving lines, vaulted brick ceilings, elaborate tile work, color, color, and more color! What I love best about the Mexican style is that nothing is exactly perfect, which is a wonderful by-product of something truly handmade.

A traditional Mexican style home is very addicting. Although I own an early American Bungalow that will be fully furnished with my own handmade Arts & Crafts furniture, I cannot help but wonder which room is going to get the full Mexican style treatment!

Enjoy!

Contents

Opposite: A patio in the open air provides a delightful view of San Miguel. *Estrella de la Mañana.*

Landscaping in Dry Climates

The following interview was recorded with Frank Stryker, owner of Silverbell Nursery; and Sparky Heinig, Arizona Certified Nursery Professional, Certified Arborist, and General Manager of the nursery; in Tucson, Arizona, December 28, 2001.

Tucson receives approximately twelve inches of rain annually, with eight of those inches falling in their summer monsoon season. Average humidity is twenty-five percent. Annual rainfall in San Miguel de Allende, Mexico, reaches about twenty inches, sixteen of those in their summer monsoon season. Average humidity there is forty percent.

McMenamin— With San Miguel and Tucson having similar dry climates, and most of their annual rainfall coming with the summer monsoon season, it is easy to understand why both cities have closely related Xeriscapes (low-water-demanding landscaping). Can you tell us a little about the concept of Xeriscape?

Stryker— Xeriscape is the idea that the land surrounding the home is divided into distinctly different areas, with each one having its own purpose. Areas that are distanced from *portales* and outdoor *salas*, adjacent to the elevations, and beyond perimeter walls are generally considered low maintenance with low water use plantings. As you enter into the courtyards, patios, and swimming pool areas, they become lusher, more intensive in their maintenance and consequently use more water. We also find that within Xeriscaping there are generally a lot of potted plants and I think that over a period of years that flower gardening has become more concentrated in containers, rather than in the ground. Generally, I would say that Xeriscaping—the management of water and using appropriate materials in the right locations—gives people the opportunity to live in a greener environment without having large expanses of lawn, which are on their way out here in the desert. Moreover, I think that within Xeriscape, that you will find a much higher use of waterfalls and fountains, much more so than ever in the past.

McMenamin— It is interesting that you would mention fountains and waterfalls as it relates to Xeriscape because every *casa* we photographed included at least one fountain and I can think of one that included a water-

fall. Aside from the fact that *fuentes* are a *must have* detail in Mexican style homes, they really add a relaxing element to the surrounding dry desert environment, would you agree?

Stryker— Absolutely. As I recall, from classes I took a long time ago when studying about the Moors conquering Portugal and southern Spain, the Moors were coming from an environment where there was no water. They started building waterworks everywhere—right through their houses. There are pictures of old Spanish houses that had just a little tiled waterway coming all the way through the house. It was the kind of extravagance the Moors had never known and I think that entire concept (the use of water) came from Spain to Mexico. An awful lot of what we see here in Tucson's Mexican architecture goes all the way back to the Moors and the effects they had.

McMenamin— Sparky, what are your thoughts on Xeriscape?

Heinig— I would like to add that utilizing Xeriscape does not limit your potential for what you can plant in your landscape. When I came here twenty years ago, I fought Xeriscape and put in large perennial beds, but I learned very quickly that was not the way to go. If you choose your plant palette carefully, you can have color in your garden almost twelve months out of the year—working with Mother Nature as opposed to against her.

Stryker— I think that is probably one of the main concepts behind Xeriscaping. I think that the jury is still out as to whether or not Xeriscaping actually accomplishes its goals. Xeriscape is a concept that applies all over the world; it is just not a Southwestern thing. As to whether or not we actually do real water savings using Xeriscape, sometimes I wonder.

Heinig— Would you say that is because of over-attentive planting, planting too much in any given area, things like that?

Stryker— Certainly, but also I do not think that irrigation systems are monitored properly. Theoretically, after a period of some years, it would be possible to shut off the irrigation system to some plantings. That is, if owners wean the plants off in a proper fashion, but most homeowners do not do that. The houses that we see and

Opposite: Color on exterior elevations is an important aspect commom to Mexico's Spanish Colonial *casas*. Not only does color serve the purpose of delineating property lines, but it leaves no doubt as to the Mexican's profuse love affair with color. The charming Spanish Colonial city of Guanajuato is an excellent example illustrating Mexico's infatuation with color.

work on, as well as the people that we sell plants to, well, I am not sure how water conscious they are. I think that the average new home today probably uses at least as much water, gallon wise, as the homes built thirty years ago.

McMenamin— Sparky, do you have any closing thoughts on Xeriscape?

Heinig— Just take full advantage of it by incorporating native plant materials where possible and what you do not know, certainly get into the nursery and educate yourself about it.

McMenamin— Mexican houses, with their open courtyards, pools, and *portales* seem to dictate a certain genre of plants. Obviously a pine tree would look a little out of place with these architectural gems, so using common names where possible, what are some of the plants that you could recommend that would enhance and compliment the architecture? A good place to start might be with the exterior perimeter walls and against the elevations.

Heinig— Well, that is where I encourage the use of native plant materials. We can use those that are already there, ones that can be brought and brokered in, planted and nurtured along, and eventually irrigated only occasionally. I think it is here that we blend our garden into the native vegetation around it. Therefore, I would certainly encourage the use of native plant materials there— small trees and shrubs, agaves, yuccas—whatever the case may be in relation to the homeowners' area.

McMenamin— Besides agaves and yuccas, what else would work?

Stryker— Larger yuccas and agaves, ocotillos, saguaros, cereus aloe, desert spoon, and nolina—those sorts of plants that we consider to be accent plants. The backbone plants of all of this would be shade trees of some sort—because you have to have shade in the desert. In the last fifteen years, we have seen the rising popularity of the hybrid varieties of mesquite, palo verdes, acacias, and Texas ebony. Some of these plants are rapid growing, while some are not, and that fact tends to make up someone's mind quickly as to what they want. That is why you see so many acacias and mesquites being planted because they are rapid growing trees and generally, drought tolerant. However, you can certainly give them more water if they need it.

McMenamin— Moving into the inner courtyards, what are some suggestions for this area?

Heinig— Well, I think that there are countless options, depending on the individual's taste. In my own courtyard, I want to see color and lushness. Attracting nature is a popular sentiment in Arizona and if you like hummingbirds, for example, we can find a plethora of plants that they prefer—like red salvias and Mexican honeysuckle. Two good choices for butterflies are lantanas and buddleias.

Stryker— I would say that when you get into a courtyard situation you are talking about a part of the Xeriscape concept known as microclimates. For example, a courtyard area is totally different from the other side of the perimeter wall, underneath the mesquite tree, or other side of the house, because you are talking about temperatures that are much warmer. (Other examples of a microclimate would be underneath overhangs or a two, three, or four-sided patio where the heat radiates from the walls all night long). And the warmer the microclimate—the palette of plant material, suitable for containers, expands. So, within microclimates, you just have an amazing amount of plant material that you can grow there, but could not grow just thirty feet away outside the wall. That is the reason why your readers will see an infinite variety of plants around the courtyards. Two plants that appear frequently in your photos are geraniums and petunias; they are somewhat bulletproof and dependable. However, the idea of growing annuals in pots is also a good one. There are winter annuals that tolerate the cold and summer annuals that can take the heat. Each has a life span of about six to eight months, which means that twice a year you trash the dead ones and re-plant giving you those twelve months of color.

Heinig— Complemented by perennials that have shorter bloom seasons or plants that have strong silhouettes or structural appearances, I think.

Stryker— Again, that would be agaves and palms.

McMenamin— There seems to be an extensive use of container plants on the *portales* and patios of Mexican style homes. Can you give us some ideas as to what plants work well in containers?

Stryker— More and more, I think, appropriately are the accent plants—yuccas, agaves, and aloes. Aloes are certainly just incredibly striking in contrast to almost anything. The essence of patios and *portales* is COLOR and not necessarily from flowers, but with the colors of the walls. The Mexican use of color is incredible and that is a big part of the warm feeling that you get from these homes. Interestingly, the shades of the incredibly vibrant colors have to do with flowers.

McMenamin— We have seen numerous color combinations of purple, yellow, green, red, orange, and pink. In your opinion, is there any problem using all of these vibrant colors together?

Stryker— Not at all.

Heinig— Not in my mind either. Never rule out color and texture, all of these things add elements as well. I mean, just a single potted cereus against a beautifully colored wall can make or break a given part of the garden, so flowers are not everything, but then we get back to annuals. There is a color or flower shape for everyone. It is just a matter of getting out and educating yourself as to what you like, what you do not like and through experimentation, you may eventually just settle on four or five flowers that you use for the rest of your life because those species work well. Just plant what you enjoy!

McMenamin— When you meet with a homeowner to discuss their landscaping needs, you certainly must make suggestions as to the types of plants that would complement the area. Nevertheless, what do you do if the owner expresses a desire for specific colors; say for instance that they want all pink. Do you accommodate the owner and plant lots of pink material?

Stryker— Absolutely. They might say, I hate red, do not give me any red. That happens a lot.

Heinig— I tell homeowners to use plants with colors that they prefer. If that means orange and purple, then use those colors. It is their space and I am a firm believer in using color!

Stryker— One interesting thing too is that in the vast majority of the installations that we do, we try not to get involved in picking out pots or flowers. In the majority of photos presented here, there most certainly is a gardener involved. It might be a family member or a paid employee, but flowers need attention. I have visited so many homes where the installation of ten pots, housing ten different plants and flowers, could change the environment 100%, but if the owners are not gardeners or they do not have one, they are not going to add them. They are going to end up with something that is going to look somewhat more sterile, not as inviting and relaxing.

McMenamin— If the homeowners do not have a gardener, but want to have a lush landscape, is there any advice that you can give them?

Stryker— Come in and talk to us, other people, or go visit their nursery. There are all sorts of programs that are set up by the extension agencies that teach homeowners how to be a flower gardener or vegetable gardener, and there are many books on the subject.

Heinig— I tell people to tap into their resources. One of Tucson's best resources is the Arizona-Sonora Desert Museum. When new homeowners come to see me, the first thing I tell them is to look around and see what appeals to them. They can also bring small samples of plants they like and we can tell them where it will work in the landscaping or if it will work at all. Oftentimes, it can be disappointing to homeowners when I point out that the particular tree they want is going to reach a height of twenty-five feet and spread fifteen feet across when they were actually looking for just a five-foot tree.

McMenamin— So unless our homeowners are professional gardeners, it might be beneficial initially to work with a professional because as you point out, mistakes can be costly and full of surprises.

Heinig— I would suggest that owners know their property and have questions lined up when they visit the nursery. If they do not get the answers that they need, then they are in the wrong nursery and should look elsewhere. The bottom line is—this is their living space and working with a professional certainly is a good idea.

McMenamin— Thanks to both of you for your valuable insights into desert landscaping and all that it entails. As the readers will see as they peruse this book, it is possible to have beautiful gardens in a desert environment!

Chapter 1
Facades- *Fachadas*

The beauty of the Mexican style home begins with the facade and whether in Mexico or the States, the facades share quite a few common characteristics. The home's layout is usually in an L or U shape and designed around many *portales*/patios that are delineated by arcades, columns, posts, or pillars. Quatrefoil windows and niches may be employed to break up a large expanse of wall and lend a striking effect. Roofs are normally flat and may include interesting parapet treatments or *cantera* stone trim. Mission tile (*teja*) adorns sloped overhangs that work in conjunction with exterior finishes in stucco, mortar-washed block, brick, or stone rubble.

However, the "street" facade can differ greatly on each side of the border. In Colonial Mexican cities, like San Miguel, we often see high fortress-like walls extending along the property lines, which totally obscure the home's facade. Homeowners paint these walls with *Cal* (lime-wash paint) in a contrasting color from their neighbor.

Not only does this practice provide the rainbow colored streets seen all over Mexico, but it further delineates property lines and helps visitors find the home easily. Elevations behind these walls, the "interior" elevations, receive an abundance of architectural details including *cantera* stonework, arcades, *portales*, fountains, fireplaces, swimming pools, and the lavish gardens—all hidden behind the "street" facade. Therefore, unless visitors receive an invitation to pass beyond the exterior walls, the beauty of these homes remains illusive.

Contrarily, in the States, the "street" facade exposes much of the home's exterior elevations along with its architectural details. While these homes may also have perimeter walls, they are usually constructed at a relatively low height; allowing passersby the opportunity to appreciate the intricate details and resulting curb appeal of the home.

The original Indian weathervane, above the Mission tile roofed tower, continues to sway with the wind, even today. A bricked pathway leads to the front door that is flanked by a Mexican fencepost cactus on the left, and a Peruvian tree cactus on the right. *El Castillo.*

Opposite page:
Plastered walls in a mellowed mustard tint are a perfect background color for the cobalt awnings and red Mission tile roof. One of Tucson's most renowned architects, Josias T. Joesler, designed this 1932 Spanish home, whose charm and beauty are as delightful today as it was when it was built. *El Castillo.*

Bandidos would think twice before trying to steal this iron house sign that is intermingled among the cholla. *El Castillo.*

A pot of gazanias sits on the low profile plastered wall that borders the walkway leading away from the front door to the outdoor *sala* and pool area, via the archway. A large sago palm and varieties of euphorbia enrich the home's architectural lines. *El Castillo.*

Saguaros and barrel cactus stand like sentries alongside the perimeter walls. The yellow trumpet vine, or cat's claw, clings to the rooftop. *El Castillo*.

In 1999, a new outdoor *sala* was added. It maintains the architectural integrity of the original home and it is virtually impossible to distinguish the original structure from the new addition—a credit to the owners and architect. Two varieties of palms, sago and pony tail, flank the window. *El Castillo*.

A stunning two-story, sun-lit facade was constructed with a winning trio of rock, painted plaster, and *cantera* surrounds. An iron balustrade lines the entry level and is covered with geraniums, bougainvillea, potted aloes, and a Virginia creeper. *Casa del Parque.*

Left:
To the left of the front door, *talavera* tiles proclaim the home's particulars. *Casa de la Cuesta.*

Left:
The lack of weathering paint on the *fachada frontal* is the only clue indicating that this home might be newly constructed. The two-story facade exhibits a large pair of garage doors, two door balconies, and an entry door next to the niche. A parade of potted fountain grass perches on the roof's edge. *Casa de la Cuesta.*

The turret *(torre)*, with its tiled *cúpula*, contains a spiraling staircase that provides access to the second floor's gallery and bedroom. The glassed doorways supply the rooms with lots of natural lighting. A potted bougainvillea rests on a pedestal over the iron railing. *Casa de la Cuesta.*

Left:
The interior elevations begin at the end of the passageway from the strret to the inner courtyard *(zaguán)*. A vivid pink two-story, U-shaped structure flows around the central courtyard and fountain. The fountain is set against a dividing common wall, which effectively encloses the home totally. Pink *cantera* stone columns form the lower level arcade and line the upper *corredor*. *Casa de la Cuesta.*

The front elevation—**before**. According to the owners, this home was overrun with rattlesnakes, packrats, bees, and termites when they bought it in 1991. But their vision, perseverance, and the help of a good architect transformed it into the show-stopper that it is today. *Red Thunder Ranch.* Photograph courtesy of the owners.

The existing grass lawn was removed and replaced with native desert landscaping, including saguaros, Texas rangers, prickly pear, cassias, and agaves. A new master suite (right side) was added, complete with a fireplace and a porch *(portal)*. The four iron overhang supports, seen on the old front porch, dated the home and were replaced with more traditional wooden posts. And what a difference a new coat of paint made! Paint: Dunn Edwards® Mayan. *Red Thunder Ranch.*

New front steps were installed with flagstone, which continues upwards to the *portal* and around the pool area. The metal art sculpture was found in Santa Fe. *Red Thunder Ranch.*

The rear elevation—**before**. See page 23 for the **after** view.
Red Thunder Ranch. Photograph courtesy of the owners.

The flagstone flooring synchronizes with the painted stucco beautifully. Iron rings mounted on the stair railing are a typical Spanish decorative touch and a customary method of hanging flowerpots. On the roof is the meditation room and unbelievable panoramic vistas. *Red Thunder Ranch*.

Flagstone flooring superceded the grass, and new paint and the addition of a *cantera* fountain dramatically transformed the rear elevation. *Red Thunder Ranch.*

Reminiscent of a Mission style fortress, this home's facade is an interesting union of natural and painted rock. *Talavera* tile was installed on the stair risers and the *cúpula* at the rear roof. Extensive *cantera* stone work trims the doorways and *cornisa*. *Casa de Hernández.*

A *citarilla* (balustrade) shapes the parapet treatment along the roof of this L-shaped front elevation, further enhanced by finials and an *espadaña* (raised archway). Three arches surround the main entrance, and the Mission tile roofing is supported by pine Tarascan posts. The perimeter walls exhibit the same *citarilla* design. *Casa del Sol y Luna.*

The rear elevation is a modified L-shape extending in a different direction than the L on the front elevation. The *citarilla*, a partnership of block and *teja,* works beautifully with the Mission tile roof that ends in block pillars. The arched bell tower is referred to as an *espadaña* and was hand-formed by one of the masons, using only a piece of wire to guide him. It is adorned by an iron *reja*. This site, located high in the mountains, has 180-degree city and mountain vistas on this side of the home. The architect emphasized the magnificent views through long, spanning *portales* and the incorporation of eight arched, double casement windows and three pair of French doors. *Casa del Sol y Luna.*

Alongside the outer gate, this *talavera* plaque reads, "*Bienvenidos a la Casa de Sol y Luna.*" *Casa del Sol y Luna.*

A sun sets on this charming and quaint home outside San Miguel's historic district. The thick mustard color stone walls, trimmed with Indian red paint, are topped by Mission roof tile. The owner was asked about the age of the house, but it remains a secret, even to her. The thickness of walls has always been a clue to dating old houses in Mexico, and these walls are several feet thick, indicating it is well over a hundred years old. The beautiful surrounding landscape is a myriad of aloes, hearts and flowers (as ground cover under the tree), hibiscus, geraniums, and vinca. *La Haciendita*.

Right:
The home's name and address were hand-painted on the *talavera* house sign, located to the left of the front door. *Villa Scorpio al Puente*.

This street facade, with its wonderfully worn mustard color paint, is appropriately adorned with iron lanterns, *cantera* door surrounds, and the ever-present projecting *canales*. The high walls resemble old Spanish fortresses. Pots of geraniums and periwinkles add a dash of color along the rooftop. *Villa Scorpio al Puente*.

This view from the entrance passageway (*zaguán*) demonstrates a classic Spanish Colonial home built around a central patio. The majority of the living area is on the second floor. *Villa Scorpio al Puente*.

Opposite page:
Moving further into the courtyard, one can see extensive work in
cantera stone in the door surrounds, the *corona* (crown) underneath
the second floor mesquite doors, the courtyard flooring, and the
fountain. Bougainvillea spills over the thirty-foot-high walls and a
huge philodendron reaches for the sky. *Villa Scorpio al Puente.*

A climb to the rooftop here reveals a breathtaking vista of San Miguel de Allende. If standing near the edge
provokes a squeamish stomach, all of the glorious details can be viewed sitting under the covered *portal* at the
left. *Villa Scorpio al Puente.*

Curved masonry walls surround the inner courtyard of this home's front elevations. Both revival and Mission influences are apparent in the arched windows and walls, niches, and varying levels of Mission tiled roofs. Accenting the space are desert spoons, yucca, lantana, cereus, and a sweet acacia tree. Paint: Dunn-Edwards® Fawn. *Casa de Moser.*

The rear elevation gathers the morning sun and guests staying in the second floor bedroom have their own porch *(portal)* from which to view incredible Arizona sunrises. The patio door, at ground level, leads into the kitchen. *Casa de Moser.*

At the other end, patio doors from the Great room and master suite yield access to the porch, pool, spa, and gardens. *Casa de Moser*.

The front facade (*fachada exterior*) is punctuated by the *cantera* door and window embellishments and the old brick on the roof. Narrow cobblestone streets are sure and constant reminders that San Miguel is a colonial city. *Casa de Roberts*.

A Virginia creeper vine winds up and across the street facade, while bougainvilleas are beginning to crest the parapet. *Casa Chorro*.

Although a three-story home is unusual in San Miguel, the interior elevations preserve the Mexican style of architecture. *Cantera* columns support the Mission tiled roof overhangs; arched windows and doors are encased in *cantera*, and there is an expansive *corredor* and balcony on the second and third levels. Potted plants sit everywhere: on the rooftops, railings, and grounds. Some of the plant species include an Australian tree fern, Boston fern, cypress tree, geraniums, creeping fig, Mexican sage bush, and a huge gunnera. *Casa Chorro.*

Right:
The guest bedrooms are located in a totally separate structure, but its facade is a mirror image of the main house. The iron railing, running along the half-arch stairway, holds pots of geraniums, and a Virginia creeper vine meanders along the lower balustrade. *Casa Chorro.*

The roof's pergola and the *cantera* trim of the roofline further highlight the street facade with its washed blue wall and contrasting painted dado. A variety of plants are in evidence on the open terrace, including jasmine, oleanders, and angels trumpet. *Casa de Reinhart.*

The side elevation exhibits a unique blending of contemporary and traditional architectural elements inspired by the style of well-known Mexican *arquitecto*, Luis Barragán. The contemporary straight lines of the walls are juxtaposed with the traditional quatrefoil window, volcanic rock wall, and *petatillo* brick pathways. A showy display of plant material includes roses, hibiscus, rosemary, society garlic, and geraniums. *Casa de Reinhart.*

Another view illustrates the stone flooring and angle of the stairway. *Casa de Reinhart*.

Opposite page:
It boggles the imagination to think of the area seen in this photograph and the next one as it used to be; a parking lot for a youth hostel that was crammed with trailers. A short stroll from the main courtyard, via the stone arches, you find a portion of the incredible transformation. This view focuses on the corner outdoor kitchen *(cocina)* and small patio above it. *Casa de la Condessa.*

Right:
The opposing view, away from the outdoor *cocina*, looks across the pool *(alberca)* into the home's second outside living room. A *cantera* stairway, in the left corner, ascends to the second floor of the home. Lush landscaping softens the facade and the popular *medio-pañuelo* tile, in both herring-bone and sawtooth designs, adds another colorful dimension to the pathways. *Casa de la Condessa.*

As with most Spanish Colonial homes in San Miguel, different wall colors delineate property lines. The simple terracotta *fachada exterior* in no way prepares you for the incredible beauty that lies just beyond the front door. Note the blue and white tiled chimney. *Casa de la Condessa.*

From the front door, a few steps through the *zaguán* brings you to the interior courtyard that services the U-shaped home. An arcaded *portal* shelters one of the home's two outdoor living rooms (*salas*). Above the arch on the left side, a glimpse of the second floor's *citarilla* may be seen. Ferns, philodendrons, and geraniums contribute to the inviting surroundings. *Casa de la Condessa*.

Left:
The new addition includes a Mission style roof arch (*espadaña*) housing a *cantera* lion. A plaster relief surrounds the front door that is trimmed with *talavera* tile. The parapet treatment, a mix of clay roof tile (*teja*) and block, along with pre-cast concrete finials and *canales,* provides additional decorative details. *Casa de Ghinis.*

Below:
Sprawling across the desert below the Santa Catalina mountains, this home's front elevations are strikingly beautiful with their different levels, many angles, and parapet treatment of brick and clay tile (*teja*). Plastered white walls rise to a Mission tile roof and a dome covered in cobalt blue *talavera* tiles. This is a good example of a home that complements the land. It rests amid the natural beauty of the Sonoran desert that is filled with saguaros, foothills palo verdes, and creosote bushes. *Casa de Wachs.*

Exiting the passageway from the street *(zaguán)*, visitors land in the central courtyard and catch a first glimpse at the interior elevations. Here, *cantera* columns rise to support the arches of the pink plastered walls. The outdoor living room *(sala)* and its entryway have an infusion of potted plants, including pigmy palms, ferns, and airplane plants. *Estrella de la Mañana.*

Fast climbing pink trumpet vine cloaks the right side of the facade. Additionally, there is an interior garden, at the back of the *sala*, with a stone wall. The courtyard floor is laid in an interesting checker-board pattern of rock and stone. Originally the floor was stone and grass, but the grass did not receive enough sunlight to grow, so it was pulled out and replaced by the rocks. *Estrella de la Mañana.*

Built in 1902, the front elevation of this Mission style home includes a centered quatrefoil window and wrap-around arcaded *portal*. Several varieties of colorful bougainvillea climb the plastered white walls, while palm trees line the sides of the home. *Allison/Henry Trost House*.

Right:
A side elevation displays a brick-trimmed quatrefoil window and brick cornice. *Allison/Henry Trost House*.

This hilltop site was, at times, a formidable opponent for the owners and architect. An extraordinary amount of rock was uncovered during grading, of which 90% was cut and recycled back into the home, including both the exterior and retaining walls and the exceptional, massive, round *pilar*. *Cantera* stone balusters wrap the open terrace along the main level of the home. Two door balconies, along with a pair of quatrefoil windows, add to the striking symmetry of the elevations. The profuse coloring, above the retaining wall, is a by-product of planting several varieties of bougainvillea together. *Casa Heyne*.

From the second floor *corredor*, we see another angle of the waterfall and the west interior elevation. *Cantera* arches and a row of *canales* frame the windows above the Mission tile roof that overhangs the *portal*. *Casa Heyne*.

A glimpse of the north side elevation shows a row of overflowing clay pots filled with geraniums and ferns that line the second floor *corredor*. *Cantera* stone trims the parapet, and the chimney ends in arches that mirror those over the windows. Ornamental date palms, lily of the Nile, and asparagus ferns surround the fish pond. The whole ambiance screams "let's do it *mañana*." *Casa Heyne*.

The home's interior elevations are in the classic U-shaped design, wrapping around a central courtyard. Exiting the *zaguán*, the two remaining sides of the U-shape are visible. *Casa Heyne.*

The east facade includes a *talavera* tiled stairway leading to the second floor. The south side has a high masonry wall that culminates in a waterfall made from huge boulders uncovered on site. Many varieties of palms, ferns, and flowers help to create the natural appearance. *Casa Heyne*.

Separate from the main house are two additional structures, a home office (far right) and the *portal*. Having the home office in a separate structure insures privacy and a very short office commute, all the while enjoying the saguaro, blue palo verde, desert spoon, yucca, aloe folia, and Texas mountain laurel. *Casa de Alegret*.

Left:
The low profile walls in the foreground, surrounding the open courtyard, have been painted the same color as the home and topped off with a contrasting color, which adds interest. Mexican terracotta pots are filled with a variety of cactus, ferns and mixed annuals. Paint: Dunn-Edwards® Terracotta formula. *Casa de Alegret*.

If in doubt as to your whereabouts, just check at the front gate, where the pyracantha is trimmed back to reveal the home's name. *La Casa Lomita Linda*.

Right:
A new wall, complementing the original elevations, incorporates faux painted iron art made locally by artist Steven Derks. *La Casa Lomita Linda*.

Left:
The solidity of the brick pillars, interspersed with large pots filled with yucca and Mediterranean fan palms, exudes Old World charm at the front of this home. A weathered wooden pergola, dripping with Carolina jasmine, further adds a relaxing atmosphere. *La Casa Lomita Linda.*

Below:
San Miguel de Allende was home for many years before the owners of this new *casa* moved to Tucson. Their design shows plenty of old Mexican influence, including the recessed shell above the covered entry, *cantera* stone columns, and loads of potted plants and bougainvillea. *Casa de Robinson.*

Under the blue Arizona sky and silhouetted against the Catalina Mountains, the different planes of this front elevation cast shadows to create an indelible impression to those appraching from the circular drive. The centuries-old tradition of using *cantera* stone for cornices, surrounds, and other architectural features with the plastered walls insures that this home will never date itself. *La Flor del Desierto*.

A partial view of the home's rear elevation reveals elegant simplicity in Spanish design, focusing on the *cantera* cornices along the roof and the *cantera*-lined arcade. To the left of the two story section, another arcade continues. *La Flor del Desierto*.

Left:
The guest house (back right) mimics the architectural details of the main house perfectly. A variety of plant material, including sago palms, desert petunias, hibiscus, burford holly, and geraniums, provide color while the mesquite tree contributes welcome shade. *La Flor del Desierto*.

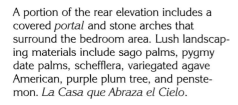

Embedded into the plaster over the threshold, a *talavera* plaque proclaims that you are entering *La Casa que Abraza el Cielo*.

A portion of the rear elevation includes a covered *portal* and stone arches that surround the bedroom area. Lush landscaping materials include sago palms, pygmy date palms, schefflera, variegated agave American, purple plum tree, and penstemon. *La Casa que Abraza el Cielo*.

A spa was creatively placed between the arcaded mud adobe and stone surrounds, reminiscent of an early aqueduct. *La Casa que Abraza el Cielo*.

An interesting array of *cantera* sculptures parade on the low profile walls that lead to the front door. Mission tile caps the chimneys and overhang, while alternating shades of brick cover the courtyard floor in a herringbone pattern. Thriving in the landscaping are examples of Mediterranean fan and queen palms, along with desert myrtle, variegated yucca gloriosa, and potted geraniums. *Casa Kino*.

The owner used Autoclaved Aerated Concrete for wall material. The specs on this material include high insulation, more flame retardant than brick or block, no insect penetration, and the ability to cut easily for shaping and contouring. While stucco is normally the outside finish, it is also possible to plaster these walls inside. Garden delights include juniper, organ pipe cactus, mammillaria cactus, nandina, and oleanders. *Casa Kino*.

Two Mission tile roofed *portales* are supported here by plastered pillars and joined by a flagstone walk. An extensive use of plant material, both in the ground and in containers, includes queen palm, philodendron, varieties of yucca, purple plum, and a banana tree. *Casa Kino.*

Opposite page:
A rising tower at the front facade beckons visitors to the main entrance (*entrada principal*) with its *cantera* door and window surrounds. Two of Mexico's favorite primary colors, red and yellow, have been used together beautifully with the Mission tile roof and the painted adobe walls. Several different levels of gardens are filled with coco palms, rocio, philodendrons, bird of paradise, hibiscus, agapanthus, day lilies, asparagus ferns, and bamboo. A large mesquite tree branches out from a raised, circular brick planter. *Casa de Reiner y Gray.*

Cantera columns support a Mission tile overhang the full length of the *portal* at the rear of this home. Several different, but complementary, stones were used. The *portal*'s low profile wall was covered with a common stone and the flooring is comprised of large pavers bordered by river rock. Windows and French doors assure plenty of natural lighting inside the home and afford views of the magnificent gardens bursting with Washingtonia palms, bougainvillea, yucca, Mexican primrose, Mexican salvia, lavender, pittosporum, and native succulents. *Casa de Reiner y Gray.*

Framed by *cantera* above the front door, this *talavera* sign hints at the owners' love for dogs. *Casa de los Perros.*

Right:
The *zaguán* here exits into a small courtyard, with steps leading up to bedrooms, gardens, and the *portal*. An interesting and versatile display of Mexican roofing construction elements includes a vault (*bóveda*), clay (*teja*) roof, bricked chimney, and the utilization of volcanic rocks. Potted geraniums line the stone wall. *Casa de los Perros.*

Below:
Following the fortress style of high walls, this front exterior is awash with old faded mustard-color paint. Both windows are fronted with iron *rejas*. The door, cornice, and windows are all trimmed with *cantera* stone. *Casa de los Perros.*

Chapter 2
Doors- *Puertas*

In 1927, Rexford Newcomb, an American architect who wrote extensively about Spanish architecture, had this to say about doorways. "The doorway has from time immemorial been the one feature into which the householder has written the measure of that hospitality with which he greeted his friends." Further, he states, "The Spanish doorway may be the simplest "slot in the wall" or have the most lavish of Baroque enframements."

Both interior and exterior doors in the Mexican style home portray more of the *casa's* architectural detailing and individuality. Pine is a much-used wood, easily carved, and may be painted or stained. Further, the use of hand-forged iron adornments, in the form of *clavos* or strapping is commonplace. *Cantera* stone or *talavera* tile often surrounds the exterior doors, which further enhances their beauty.

Designed by a friend of the owners, the home's eight-foot high, double, pine doors were commissioned and hand carved in Mexico. To complement the door, mustard yellow *talavera* tiles alternate with cobalt blue in a star motif and are set at a forty-five degree angle. *Casa del Sol y Luna.*

Opposite page:
Delineated by black iron straps, this handsomely carved front door's interior side depicts men and women playing musical instruments. *Santos* figures, displayed on the cupboard alongside, keep an eye on those coming and going. *Casa de Franklin.*

Carved in 1983 by Frank Franklin, the exterior side of the front door is uniquely inscribed with the following: *tristeza, cariño, canción,* and *pajarito. Casa de Franklin.*

Ocher walls with contrasting trim highlight the back door that was carved by Frank Franklin. Interestingly, old pine beams, discovered beneath the original termite-eaten wood flooring, supplied Franklin's lumber for all of this home's doors. *Casa de Franklin.*

Spindled double doors, which are almost hidden from view by the overhanging creeping fig vine, grant access to the garage from the front courtyard. The carved stone pot is from the state of Sonora. *Casa de Alegret.*

A charming floral frieze around the salvaged and restored front door warrants closer inspection, but stop along the way to admire the hibiscus tree, boxwood, and photinia. *Casa de Alegret*.

Curvilinear Mexican clay pots and a *cantera* surround balance the bas-relief doors at this home's main entrance. An iron chandelier and a pair of iron sconces cast delicate shadows across the threshold. *La Flor del Desierto*.

An unusual and beautiful combination of glass and turned wooden spindles creates a captivating front door that permits natural light to filter into the home. *Casa de Moser*.

Opposite page:
Deeply carved into this pine door from Michoacán is a 1950s rendition of the Sun and Moon motif. It offers a strong hint that something special awaits visitors just inside this front door. *Casa de Ghinis.*

Right:
A pair of sumptuous pine front doors—hand carved and studded with black iron *clavos* and strapping—are encompassed by *cantera* stone. The fine workmanship in the wrought iron transom and iron bars is indeed the work of a *maestro. Casa Heyne.*

Made by Abundio Fierro, the garage doors mimic the front door's design, with the exception of the transom. *Casa Heyne.*

Opposite page:
A multi-paneled, carved pine door adorned with black iron leads to the owners' private *casita*. A potted hibiscus and large *talavera* jar add color to the entrance. *Casa de la Cuesta.*

Rusted to perfection is this pair of iron arched doors made locally by Old Pueblo Ironworks. A beautiful door for a utility room! *Casa de Alegret.*

There is something very special about using old doors at front entrances. This pair of eleventh century Moroccan doors is coupled with a *cantera* stone surround and an iron transom. *Casa Chorro.*

An intricately designed, hand-forged iron arbor will support climbing white roses. In the meantime, it stands as a work of art surrounding the French doors. *Casa Heyne*.

A nice pair of carved and geometric paneled doors, complete with a *postigo*, an iron door knocker *(llamador)*, a letter slot, and *cantera* surround, proclaim this front entrance. *Casa de Reinhart*.

This pair of carved *padre* doors enlivens the front passageway *(zaguán)* and is particularly compatible with Mexican paintings offering thanks *(exvotos)* that hang on the wall. *Casa de los Perros*.

Unusual, one of a kind doors often are the by-product of the owner's imagination. This carved door was commissioned to harmonize with the *cantera* fireplace in the home's living room. *Casa de los Perros*.

Doors throughout Mexico provide inspiration to homeowners in the United States, as was the case with this eight-foot, alder wood door that is adorned with iron straps and nails *(clavos). Casa de Robinson.*

These carved pine, interior doors have pre-cast concrete surrounds. The electrifying faux-painted walls brighten the hallway. Paint: Dunn-Edwards® Ocotilla. *Casa de Ghinis.*

All of this home's eight-foot high, solid pine interior doors were custom designed and fabricated by 4 Brothers Cabinetry in Tucson. Black iron *clavos*, L-brackets, and levers accentuate the overall designs. *Casa del Sol y Luna*.

Designed with a Moroccan look, this pine interior door was beautifully handcrafted by Abundio Fierro. *Casa Heyne*.

Surrounding the inside of the paneled double front door is a vibrantly hand-painted, multi-colored frieze by Lisa Mellinger. Painting friezes around the doors and windows is an age-old tradition in Mexico. *Casa de Roberts*.

Need a clever idea to dress up a plain door? Six tin panels transformed the ordinary surface into an interesting design. *Casa de la Condessa*.

This six-paneled arched door was commissioned in San Miguel and made by Salvador Orozco. *La Flor del Desierto*.

A dramatic space is created in this arched passageway by the addition of a painted dado. *Casa Heyne*.

Chapter 3
Gates- *Portones*

Owners and decorators exercise as much care in choosing appropriate gates as any other architectural component of the house. Whether forged-iron or carved wood, short or tall, gates take on many forms and personalities and add to the architectural continuity of the home.

This iron-strapped gate restrains unwanted desert critters from transcending the flagstone pathway to the backyard. *Casa de Robinson*.

An arched wrought iron gate is housed in this perimeter wall. *Casa de Ghinis.*

Salvaged building materials added important finishing touches to this home in the form of the intricately detailed iron gate. The present owners managed to save it from a Tucson mansion being torn down, and they put it to excellent use! Bougainvilleas provide the electric color. *Allison/Henry Trost House.*

The pretty blue paint on this backyard gate is accented by black iron strapping. Fern-filled pots, found in Tlaquepaque, perch on top of the wall. *Casa Kino.*

Geometric tile wainscoting leads to the pine double gate in this wall, to create a captivating exterior entrance. *Casa Kino*.

Tlaquepaque cobalt blue glass jars flank a carved pine gate. Distressed blue paint harmonizes with the iron *clavos*. *Casa Kino*.

The beautiful wrought iron serpent design in this gate marks the end of the path from a garden filled with purple verbena and weeping fig. *Casa de Alegret.*

An arched iron gate secures the pool in this garden where potted cactus and blooming bougainvilleas broadcast color against the brilliant walls. *Casa de Alegret.*

The carved pine outer gate, made by Frank Franklin, carries the following greeting, which we understand is a verse from a favorite song, *"La vida no vale nada, comienza siempre llorando y así llorando se acaba."* (Life is worth nothing, it begins with crying, and it always ends with crying). *La Casa Lomita Linda.*

An arched iron gate separates the back patios and the garage. *La Casa que Abraza el Cielo.*

A locally crafted arched and hand-forged iron gate leads to an intimate garden in the desert. *La Casa que Abraza el Cielo.*

The gate on the right opens to the outdoor living room, and the tall gate at the left, flanked by iron lamps, leads to the main entrance of the home. Foreground beds are filled with boxwood and euonymus, while pots contain petunias and pansies. A yucca and Mediterranean fan palm flank the gate. *La Casa que Abraza el Cielo*

A pair of exquisitely hand crafted iron gates, encased in massive *cantera* stone surrounds, leads to the front door. Mediterranean fan palms grow in the built-in boxes. *La Flor del Desierto*.

Left:
The first glimpse of this front courtyard is through the pair of wooden paneled gates, guarded by a euphorbia. A purple leaf plum shows off its intense color from within the courtyard walls. Paint: Dunn-Edwards® Fawn. *Casa de Moser*.

Opposite page:
To gain entrance to this home, visitors pass through the outer gate. Cat claw vines and oleanders need occasional trimming to keep them from totally shrouding it. *El Castillo*.

Opposite page:
Several layers of flaking paint cover the old Spanish Colonial doors that secure this front entrance. *Casa del Sol y Luna*.

Below:
A wrought iron gate divides and secures the patio from the *zaguán*. *Casa de la Condessa*.

Beautifully designed wrought iron double gates separate the garage from the interior space *Casa de Reinhart*.

Right:
A carved and painted gate, crafted by Frank Franklin, exudes folksy charm to the outdoor living space. *La Casa que Abraza el Cielo*.

Opposite page:
Richard Redman created the metal crowning element over Frank Franklin's carved double gate that opens into the desert. The wall-mounted metal light fixtures keep them visible at night. *La Casa Lomita Linda*.

Chapter 4
Porches and Patios-*Portales y* Patios

Outdoor living is a way of life in the desert and it is not surprising, therefore, that a major component of the Mexican house is the *portal/patio*. In fact, most of these homes are designed around the *portales*, with numerous doorways providing access to these outdoor beauties. They are always comfortably furnished and in the majority of cases, the *portales* are elaborately decorated with furnishings that would rival the best interior living rooms. Many are equipped with kitchens as well, making it easy to understand why a great deal of entertaining happens around and within the *portales*.

Pigmented mustard colored walls brighten the surroundings and set this home's first outdoor living room in a cheerful mood. Guatemalan huipiles and African mud cloth are lively upholstery fabrics on the iron furnishings. A pair of figural clay pots serve as charming table lamps that cast shadows on the bricked ceiling. *Casa de la Condessa.*

The second outdoor living room services the swimming pool area. A pair of mesquite chairs and coordinating couch are upholstered with bright green striped fabric. *Casa de la Condessa*.

Opposite page:
Moving further into this room beneath the rock stairway, a beautifully crafted pine hand-carved cupboard has been finished to look like copper. Six leather chairs, fastened with iron *clavos*, encompass the dining table. The stone flooring is from an old hacienda in Michoacán and is four inches thick. *Casa de la Condessa*.

A hand-wrought iron balustrade climbs the stairway with *cantera* treads. *Casa de la Condessa*.

Nothing beats a poolside party when all of the cooking happens close to the action. The outdoor kitchen, faced with blue and white *talavera* tile, comes equipped with a barbeque grill (*asador*) and a sink for cleanup. The chimney and cooking hood are covered in *medio-pañuelo* tile in the herringbone pattern. *Casa de la Condessa*.

Stretching to the pool area, this plant-lined patio is a tribute to the homeowner's gardening skills. *Al fresco* dining is the norm at this *casa*. *Casa de Black*.

Open doors are a beckoning signal to explore an outdoor patio with built-in benches. It is enclosed by a newly added wall. *La Casa Lomita Linda*.

Above and left:
This gigantic, L-shaped outdoor living room is equipped with a corner fireplace and several seating areas that make it a perfect place for entertaining and a welcome refuge from the sun. Potted containers filled with bird of paradise, dioon, pony tail and sago palms, and schefflera contribute to the tropical atmosphere. *La Casa Lomita Linda*.

Comfortable seating on the rear *portal* invites relaxation to enjoy this breathtaking vista. Early risers are treated to a captivating sunrise. *La Flor del Desierto*.

Opposite page:
An inner view of this sixty-by-nine-foot *portal* displays flooring of stained concrete scored at two-foot-square intervals. *Cantera* columns, archways, and door surrounds that run the entire length of the *portal's* ceiling were made onsite and installed by Garcia. Mexican clay pots, filled with sago palms and geraniums, provide harmonizing color. *La Flor del Desierto*.

Conveniently located close to the indoor kitchen, this *talavera* tiled outdoor cooking center is used often. Brightly colored fabric on the dining chairs reinforces a festive Mexican mood. *La Flor del Desierto*.

Outside the *portal*, the courtyard was laid with Kool deck, trimmed with *cantera* stone, insuring cool footing in the extreme summer heat. Two *cantera* stone, cat-shaped *canales* peer over the space. *La Flor del Desierto*.

The main level of the home is where the *corredor* connects with the living room, kitchen, and one of the bedrooms. Magical displays of indigenous folk art visually explode in every direction. *Casa de la Cuesta*.

A beam and plank ceiling and brick floors frame this magnificent forty-six-by-twenty-four-foot outdoor living room and kitchen. Adding to its warm and relaxing environment is the profuse use of plants. Some of the species seen are large potted ficus trees, bougainvillea, cereus, Christmas cactus, and euphorbia. *El Castillo*.

This portion of the outdoor kitchen, used daily, rivals the best indoor kitchens anywhere. It is completely fitted with a gas grill, double sink, dishwasher, two refrigerators, a pizza oven, microwave, and a cooktop. *El Castillo*.

Saltillo countertops make cleanup easy. Casual dining and conversations with the cook are easily accomplished from the seating at the counter. *El Castillo*.

Cushioned wicker and decorative furnishings in front of the fireplace offer comfort outdoors while the beamed ceiling protects them from the sun. The wall openings take advantage of cooling breezes. *El Castillo.*

The same space seen from the *cocina*. *El Castillo.*

Mexican pigskin-covered furnishings provide ample seating, but for a closer view of the desert, it's hard to resist the built-in benches. *Red Thunder Ranch*.

Left:
An old door was cleverly converted into a tabletop. Climate control is achieved by the fireplace or the ceiling fan, depending on the season. Paint: Dunn-Edwards® Mayan. *Red Thunder Ranch*.

Right:
An outdoor kitchen by the pool stays fully equipped for a cold drink and meal preparation. *Red Thunder Ranch*.

This home's main *portal* is fifty feet long and from twelve to twenty feet wide. A richly stained and distressed beam and plank ceiling provides relief from the hot sun, and Saltillo tile flooring remains cool and requires little maintenance. The commissioned Mexican chairs and couches include hand-carved sun and moon motifs. Cobalt blue *talavera* tile frames all of the home's French doors. Succulents, palms, ferns, and geraniums overflow *talavera* pots. *Casa del Sol y Luna. Photograph by author.*

Left:
A small side *portal* provides privacy, while the exposed aggregate concrete walkway connects the two rear *portales*. *Casa del Sol y Luna*.

The kitchen door opens directly to the outside dining room. Iron chairs, fitted with tie-back cushions, encircle a tile dining table below a ceiling fan. *Casa de Wachs*.

Mexican *talavera* tile in cobalt blue and mustard yellow forms the table top. The diamond pattern in the buffet is a *medio-pañuelo* tile design. When not being used to serve food, the buffet houses a myriad of potted plants. *Casa Kino*.

This enticing first floor outdoor living room imparts the magic of traditional Mexican homes. A cozy day bed, in front of the fireplace and under gentle breezes of the ceiling fan, creates the perfect choice for an afternoon siesta. *Estrella de la Mañana*.

This separate rooftop outdoor living area is three flights above the ground. When monsoons come to San Miguel, the owners move to the covered patio, with its built-in benches. The brick flooring has been laid in a herringbone pattern. *Estrella de la Mañana.*

Another patio, in open air, provides a delightful view of San Miguel. *Estrella de la Mañana.*

Below:
Intended for lounging, this rooftop patio is a gardener's delight. On the far wall is a *cantera*-topped iron table with a variety of succulents. Potted geraniums line the walls and an abundance of Mexican purple sage provides lively contrast. *Estrella de la Mañana.*

While pigskin-covered furniture is very comfortable as fabricated, the addition of big fluffy cushions makes it even more appealing. Doors here lead to the bedrooms. *Casa de los Perros*.

Sun-dappled afternoons are cool on this open patio. Two immense sword ferns flank the doorway and an iron arbor arches over the table. *Casa del Parque*.

The *portal's* brightly painted walls highlight and enhance the collection of Mexican folk art pottery, masks, and large Oaxacan wooden animals. In the far end niche, a sculpture entitled *Someone is Calling Someone Also* is by David Martin. *Casa de Reinhart.*

Looking from the opposite direction, it appears that this *portal* sits in the middle of a tropical rain forest. Several seating areas accommodate indelible views of the gardens. *Casa de Reinhart.*

A short stroll from the main house brings you to this outdoor kitchen. The beautifully bricked cooking area (*brasero*) uses both gas and wood fuel. The hood and flooring are made from brick laid in a herringbone pattern. Old wooden ranch furniture offers comfortable seating. *Casa Chorro*.

Here, the largest candle we have ever seen rests on the floor of the main *portal*. A dining table, sofa, and chairs insure a relaxing outdoor experience. *Casa Chorro*.

Access to a guesthouse and office is through this newly added *portal* where open arches on four sides furnish delightful garden views. The vibrant blue painted niche is electrifying against the terracotta-colored walls. The foreground is filled with Johnny-jump-ups and other potted delights, including jade plants, red fuchsias, wax-leaf privet, red rubber plant, and a palo verde tree. Paint: Dunn-Edwards® Terracotta formula. *Casa de Alegret*.

A pigskin (*equipale*) table and chairs sit conveniently beyond the door to the home's kitchen, making it easy to serve meals outside. At the opposite end, a comfortable sofa and chairs invite prolonged lingering. *Casa de Moser*.

Vintage Mission oak chairs somehow found their way to Mexico and look right at home alongside the Mexican leather and wood chairs. Pineapple clay pottery from Michoacán decks an old cupboard. *Casa de Roberts*.

Sheltered from the elements, the outside living room is the perfect place for entertaining and, on occasion, for an afternoon nap. Centered over the *chimenea* is a large Mexican *talavera* charger. *La Casa que Abraza el Cielo*.

Alongside the outdoor living room is this small open patio for casual dining. The French doors open to the formal dining room and kitchen beyond, making an easy treck for food. *La Casa que Abraza el Cielo.*

With its inviting wicker furnishings and mountain vistas, this enclosed Arizona room is a relaxing spot any time of day. A collection of vintage Mexican pottery fills the painted cupboard. *La Casa que Abraza el Cielo.*

This main *portal* is conveniently located between the living room and kitchen. All of the pigskin (*equipale*) furnishings have brightly colored Mexican fabric cushions. A dado has been painted a slightly darker shade of terracotta than the rest of the wall. *Casa Heyne*.

Forever talking and extremely animated, is this five-year-old male Mulatto Cockatoo. He spends most of the day outside his cage on the *portal. Casa Heyne*.

Pots filled with a variety of pink flowers, such as fuchsias, bougain-villea, and periwinkles, complement the vibrant pink exterior walls. *Talavera* casserole lids cover the floor facing and built-in flower beds on the left—a delightful and absolutely ingenious decorative use of discarded and broken pottery! *Casa de Salazar Olmos.*

Detail of the *talavera* lids. *Casa de Salazar Olmos*.

Chapter 5
Columns- *Columnas*

Columns, pillars, and posts are necessary structural support components that are most often used around the *portales*. They may be composed of brick, block, concrete, *cantera* stone, adobe, wood, or various combinations of these materials. The composition chosen dictates the shape, whether rounded or rectangular. Wooden posts are usually carved and capped by corbels. While the extensive use of columns is in a support role, architects and interior designers find wonderful decorative uses for them as well.

Cement-filled adobe *columnas*, bearing a heavy load, have shafts painted the same color as the exterior walls. Leaving the capitals and bases in a natural coloring further defined and enhanced them. The greenery consists of sword ferns, gardenias, and umbrella grass. *Casa Heyne.*

The owners selected a beautiful shade of natural pink *cantera* stone for their arcade and molding (*moldura de arco*). The pink seems intensifyied when coupled with the greens of fan palms and variegated airplane plants. *Casa de la Cuesta*.

A half column with symmetrical edges and a Corinthian capital has a dynamic effect against the terracotta wall. Planters are filled with chicken & hens, donkey's tail, and senecio. *Estrella de la Mañana*.

One of a pair of elegantly carved antique *cantera* stone columns found in Phoenix. The columns were fabricated in several sections, and installed together at the jobsite. *La Casa que Abraza el Cielo*.

A *cantera* arcade wraps around the *portal* that is filled with rubber trees, sago palms, shrimp plants, and geraniums. *La Flor del Desierto*.

Here brick-trimmed masonry arches spring from pillars of *cantera*. *Casa de la Condessa*.

A mortar-washed block pillar features decorative *talavera* set into a recess. Next to the pillar is a Mexican fan palm in a large Oaxacan pot. *Casa del Sol y Luna*.

Left:
Carved posts from Michoacán are usually seven to eight feet high, but here it was necessary to raise them on poured concrete pedestals to reach the lintel. The owner wanted eclipsing squares for the pattern on the pedestal, but not having any *medio-pañuelo* tiles on hand the mason cut two solid color tiles at forty-five-degree angles to achieve the same look. Yellow lantana fills a front flowerbed. *Casa del Sol y Luna*.

Some design situations require shorter posts, and cutting them down in size poses no problem. Only a section of the whole post was needed here to meet the corbel. *La Casa que Abraza el Cielo.*

A two-tiered pedestal, covered in blue and white *talavera* tile, extends this wonderfully weathered Tarascan post. *Casa de la Condessa.*

Large iron strapping secures this twist-carved post to the corbel. Potted geraniums add an infusion of color around the post. *Casa de Moser*.

Chapter 6
Fountains- *Fuentes*

The sound water emits as it trickles from a fountain is unmistakable and it further instills the relaxing environment of the Mexican style home. Three and four tier *cantera* stone fountains are installed in courtyards and/or gardens. Moreover, any exterior wall with plumbing access makes a viable candidate for a wall fountain. *Talavera* tile, with its infinite variety of motifs and colors, lends the finishing touches to the fountain basins and walls.

This *cantera* fountain basin provides birds and small desert animals with a safe haven and a ready water supply. The Mexican ceramic parrot, at water's edge, is always available for a chat with his visiting flocked friends. The fountain is nestled among lushly planted flowerbeds of pink penstemon, yellow marigolds, and red bougainvillea and salvia. *Casa de Moser*.

This front courtyard fountain hosts desert dwellers who appreciate the sight and sound of water. The built-in bench (*banco*) is an excellent place to rest and display a variety of terracotta pots. Alongside the *banco* are a purple plum tree, vinca, and jasmine. *Casa de Moser*.

This elaborate fountain was carved by Garcia, a true *cantera maestro*. The gallant lions are put to work as fountain spouts. *La Flor del Desierto*.

Left:
A recessed wall fountain, tiled in cobalt blue *talavera* and trimmed by *cantera* stone, lines one side of a *pórtico*. Water spews from the lion's mouth. *La Flor del Desierto*.

Brick and *talavera* tile (*medio-pañuelo,* eclipsing squares pattern) finished this fountain basin. The pond is alive with umbrella grass, cypress grass, and water irises. Daisies line the walkway in containers, and an olive tree provides sculptural interest and shade. *Casa de Wachs.*

Opposite page:
Added during remodeling of the courtyard, this *cantera* fountain is visible from the kitchen, bedroom, and Great room. *Red Thunder Ranch.*

Below:
Four surface treatments harmonize in this stunning wall fountain, including brick, plaster, *cantera* stone, and *talavera* tile. *Casa de Wachs.*

This meandering brick path leads through heavily planted grounds of oleanders, bougainvillea, and potted cactus to the center courtyard fountain. A continually blooming bed, filled with verbena and geraniums, encircles the fountain and benefits from the overspray. *El Castillo*.

This baptismal font was born again as a fountain basin (a good example of reusing materials) in the central courtyard. Potted geraniums girdle the fountain, a much-honored tradition in Mexico. *Casa de la Condessa*.

Opposite page:
The exposed aggregate concrete pathway splits into two directions as it passes the *cantera* fountain. A *talavera* tile basin, with a swimming fish motif, solves the problems associated with live fish. A fifteen-foot saguaro cactus survived the new construction and still stands in its original location. *Casa del Sol y Luna*.

With a little imagination, you can hear the soothing *música* played by this archangel and the swishing water at its feet. Pittosporum thrives in the background. *La Casa que Abraza el Cielo*.

Artist Elliott Meadow created an ingenious fountain for this secret garden. The boughs of the tree were executed in paint, but as the tree meanders down the wall, it becomes fully three dimensional. It certainly fools the eye among euphorbia, gardenia, and hibiscus plants. *La Casa que Abraza el Cielo*.

With Tucson's Catalina mountain range on the horizon, this fountain mimics the stately saguaro cactus in the backyard. Santa Theresa Tile Works designed and fabricated the basin and added 22-kt gold to the bird design in its sides. *Casa de Robinson.*

Water cascades from this intense red wall spout into the meandering fish pond below the stairs. *Casa de Reinhart*.

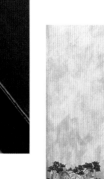

A *sapo* delivers a steady stream of water into this tiled basin. Potted fountain grass, bougainvillea, and geraniums gratefully enjoy the wet environment. *Casa de Reinhart*.

One corner of this garden holds a charming surprise. A *cantera* dog water spout sits on a *talavera* tiled pedestal in the midst of potted begonias and Mexican sage bushes. *Casa de los Perros*.

An unusual slate and tiled corner wall fountain is in this lava rock *(laja)* courtyard. A wooden Virgin of the Guadalupe doesn't seem to mind her feet being wet. At the side, a star jasmine is beginning its journey up the wall. *Casa de la Cuesta*.

An unusual, hand-carved *cantera* fountain, by Frank Franklin, divides the covered *portal* from the open courtyard. A potted dioon provides a backdrop for the figure and jasmine winds around the column to the right. *La Casa Lomita Linda*.

Stunning colored tile brings attention to this wall fountain where water flows from an old copper *canal*—an excellent idea for recycling materials. A large ocotillo provides sculptural interest behind the fountain, while gazanias, pittosporum, and geranium plants intensify the foreground. *Casa de Alegret*.

Chapter 7
Pools- *Albercas*

Pools add yet another dimension to the outdoor living concept that is so traditional to the Mexican home. In Mexico, it is prevalent to see the entire pool's interior surface covered with *talavera* tile. The beauty of the tile's vibrant colors shimmering beneath the water's surface is breathtaking. Unfortunately, due to cost, labor and other considerations, this treatment remains impractical for most homeowners in the States. However, homeowners in both countries surround their pools with comfortable chaise lounges, a variety of plants, and artistic embellishments.

The essence of Mexico is captured in the design of this negative edge pool, with a beautifully vibrant color scheme. The strategically placed prickly pear cactus insures that no one enters from the negative edge. Paint: Dunn-Edwards® Terracotta formula. *Casa de Alegret*.

This *talavera* lined pool is at home in what was once a parking lot. The painted back wall heightens the effect of the architectural stone wall behind the pool. Lava stone (*Laja*) flooring complements the *cantera* coping, while comfortable chaise lounges encourage lazy days. *Casa de la Condessa*.

An unending supply of fresh water flows into the pool from the wall-mounted lion head. Floating in this pool, while staring at the incredible Santa Catalina mountains, is pure relaxation. *Casa Kino*.

Below:
The split level design of this pool and patio area helps to define and enhance each section. Three steps lead to the elevated spa that spills water into the black-bottomed pool. To the left and back of the pool, steps lead to another sitting area. Potted annuals of pansies and marigolds, along with penstemon and bougainvillea, add lots of color to the surroundings. *Casa de Moser*.

Left:
When the owners purchased this home, the pool lacked pizzazz but was destined for a new look. *La Casa Lomita Linda. Photograph courtesy of the owners.*

Below:
The owners made no structural changes to the pool area, but what a difference the use of color makes! The spa is now an art object with the addition of murals, hand-painted by Francisco (Frank) Franklin and his daughter Maja. The front facings of the pool and planter boxes are no longer white. Sculptural native plantings complete the area and provide background for the metal sculpture by Tucson artist Steven Derks. *La Casa Lomita Linda.*

Arts abound from every direction around the negative edge pool—the huge stone heads are from Easter Island and lots of *cantera* stone animals roam freely. *La Casa Lomita Linda*.

Designed in the quatrefoil shape, the spa exhibits both solid and decorative *talavera* tiles. The ramada features built-in benches and a fireplace. *Casa de Wachs*.

Opposite page:
Three rounded steps provide entry into this pool with the beautiful *talavera* tile lining the interior. Surrounding the pool are banana trees, bougainvillea, geraniums, and lantana. *Casa Chorro.*

Pools and deserts go hand-in-hand—cooling water a necessity in surviving the desert's hot summers. Here, flagstone floors encircle a kidney-shaped pool. *Red Thunder Ranch.*

The Mission tile roof shelters an outdoor kitchen *Red Thunder Ranch.*

The dipping pool is heated by solar panels and was designed to appear as a natural body of water. It is beautifully disguised in the layer of boulders and landscaping and virtually undetectable from the main level of the home. *Casa Heyne.*

Right:
An expansive deck is around this pool. Large potted totem pole cactus, sago palms, and bougainvillea provide the alluring ambiance. *El Castillo.*

Chapter 8
Cantera Stonework- *Cantera*

Cantera is a quarry stone that is carved into an endless potpourri of shapes and forms. Use of *cantera* is limitless and since it comes in a variety of colors, it is easy for decorators and homeowners to choose a hue that will work with the home's color palette.

This regal carved *cantera* stone lion (one of a pair) guards the entrance to the home. In the background are saguaro, golden barrel cactus, and bougainvillea. *Casa de Black*.

One of the pair of guardian lions watch the step down to the pool. *Casa del Sol y Luna*.

Ever alert, a friendly-faced sitting lion welcomes visitors. *Casa Lomita Linda*.

Four ferocious lion heads protrude from this *cantera* stone pedestal. *Casa de Ghinis*.

Opposite page:
Señor Lupe Garcia, a *cantera* stone *maestro* from Guanajuato, has made all of this home's extensive *cantera* architectural details. Señor Garcia has been living onsite for three and one-half years, visiting his family every few months. With thirty-five years experience, it takes him about five hours to carve one of the cat roof *canales* and approximately two days for a column. *La Flor del Desierto*.

Found in endless shapes and sizes, *canales* drain off any water accumulation from flat roofs. The cat variety, seen here, is a product of Señor Garcia's advanced talent. *La Flor del Desierto*.

One should not overlook the possibility of using *canales* as non-functioning ornamental art. The stalking cat, one of a pair, was found in Mexico and subsequently mounted into an exterior wall. *Casa del Sol y Luna*.

At The House of the Dogs, *canales* in the shape of a dog project from the rooftop. *Casa de los Perros*.

Another dog functions as this charming fountain spout! *Casa de los Perros.*

A large and imposing *cantera* angel contributes to this garden's tranquil mood amongst oleander, cape honeysuckle, and a tree-of-heaven. *Casa de Franklin.*

Five angels watch over this home as a *cantera* carved pedestal. It could provide various functions or be left as an inspiring art object. *Casa de Black*.

An archangel on a *cantera* pedestal is shown serenely playing a violin. *Casa de Black*.

A secret garden behind carved pine doors reveals a figure of Saint Francis accompanied by a nandina shrub. *La Casa que Abraza el Cielo*.

This figure of Saint Francis is perched on a stone wall and surrounded by English ivy and hibiscus overlooking the home and gardens. *Casa de los Perros*.

Saint George (*San Jorge*) is usually depicted slaying a dragon, which stands for wickedness. Here, the entranceway to the home is protected by a figure of Saint George, one of the stone carvers' favorite subjects. *Casa de Black*.

Opposite page:
A carved figure of San Miguel stands in the center of this lava rock (*laja*) courtyard. The cut slate flooring has been laid in a radiating circular pattern. *Casa de la Cuesta*.

Mortared into a perimeter wall, a serene relief sculpture of the Virgin of the Guadalupe imparts peace and tranquility to her surroundings. *Casa de Moser*.

This carved church image *(iglesia)* can be a focal point of the landscaping. *Casa del Sol y Luna*.

This carved ram, with gentle demeanor, lies on a garden bench in front of euphorbia and an Indian fig supplies shade. *Casa de Franklin*.

A carved ram figure stands on this low wall. *Casa Kino*.

This tortise *(tortuga)* figure stands on two-color brick flooring. *Casa Kino*.

Planters can make interesting focal points. This large turtle flowerpot (*maceta*) accommodates a sago palm. *Casa de Ghinis*.

Sitting at the pool's edge, this frog (*sapo*) carving contemplates taking a dip. *La Casa Lomita Linda*.

Five carved frogs, with musical instruments, appear ready to entertain patio guests. *Casa de Black*.

Live doves visit patios in the desert naturally. This carved figure stays to ornament the garden. *Casa Kino*.

A carved *cantera* rooster figure that doesn't crow, but can greet you silently each morning. *Casa del Sol y Luna*.

A charming rabbit carving that cannot eat the garden flowers. *Casa Kino*.

Scorpions are a way of life in deserts. This carved type, however, is the only one welcome. *Villa Scorpio al Puente*.

An iguana carving provides exotic detail to the garden. *Casa de Alegret.*

As the alligator carving faces toward the pool, an iguana carving provides tension by blocking its path. *La Casa Lomita Linda.*

Another carved alligator figure poses no threat to humans, unless you try to move it. *Casa de Ghinis.*

This charming snail carving pauses along the brick wall. *La Casa Lomita Linda.*

Could this be Noah and his precious cargo? *Casa Kino.*

A lively fish carving (*pescado*) supplies a steady stream of fresh water to this pool. It is beautifully mounted before two colors of *talavera* tile. *Casa de Alegret.*

Cantera stonemasons create ornaments for every purpose. This mermaid *(sirena)* can be inserted into a wall or window opening, used as an art object, or serve as a plant pedestal. *Casa de Ghinis.*

Another lovely carved stone mermaid. *Casa de Ghinis.*

This pre-cast concrete cherub's head bracket *(ménsula)* secures an iron angel sculpture. *Casa de Ghinis.*

Placed in the home's entry courtyard, this painted figure of a kneeling woman extends a welcome (*bienvenidos*). *Casa del Sol y Luna*.

This massive sculpture of a person in a restful yoga postion sits on a raised brick pedestal behind golden barrel cactus. *La Casa Lomita Linda*.

The carved *cantera* concha shell can decorate a multitude of places as a pedestal, finial, niche ornament, or garden art. *Casa de Ghinis*.

Below:
This lovely carved and scalloped stone bowl contains multicolored glass spheres of brilliant colors, which the sunlight intensifies. *La Casa Lomita Linda*.

A carved stone radiant sun image *(el sol)* is a popular motif on traditional Mexican style walls. *Casa de Ghinis.*

Below:
Another sun-face sphere adorns this garden. *Casa Kino.*

These unusual carved stone faces appeared at a roadside stop near Delores Hidalgo. *Casa del Sol y Luna.*

A gigantic, two-by-two feet, *cantera* flowerpot *(maceta)* is carved with an unusual skull image and filled with blooming geraniums. *Casa de Reinhart*.

Is there a more fitting planter for a deset garden than this one of cactus shape? *Casa del Sol y Luna.*

An ornamental "eye of the ox" *(ojo de buey)* frame surrounds this quatrefoil window. *Casa Heyne.*

A delightful vine and climbing monkey (*chanquito*) design has been carved from stone as a ventilating window. *Casa de los Perros*.

Below:
Mexican pigskin *(equipale)* chairs deteriorate in the desert's hot sun, but this pair in carved stone take whatever abuse Mother Nature offers. *Casa de Wachs*.

Cleverly, this carved stone figure of a dozing Mexican has found a shaded place for his siesta amid the lantana and cactus. *Casa del Sol y Luna*.

Chapter 9
Gardens- *Jardines*

While the architectural details of the traditional Mexican house require no further embellishment, gardens certainly enhance the home's beauty. With the *casas* in San Miguel and Tucson residing in arid, desert terrains, a great deal of attention is focused on appropriate, drought tolerant, plant materials. Fortunately, there are incredible species from which to choose that fit these criteria. Agaves, palms, cacti, jasmine, bougainvillea, palo verde, and mesquite trees are just a few of the choices. In addition, those varieties that will not tolerate the summer heat are planted in beautiful terracotta, *cantera*, and *talavera* flowerpots and are placed under the protection of the *portales*.

In this intimate patio, a large mesquite tree grows in front of a recessed *cantera* stone fountain in the stone wall. An unusual flooring of bricks compose a sunburst pattern, and sword ferns and bamboo add to the tropical atmosphere. *Casa Heyne.*

Brightly colored *talavera* wall planters burst with a variety of succulents and flowers. In the foreground, an herb garden offers the kitchen staff with a ready supply of fresh seasonings. *Casa Heyne*.

Opposite page:
If you are remodeling and have an unwanted swimming pool, take notes. Fill the swimming pool with construction debris leaving the last two feet for a bed of concrete, add water, fish, and foliage; *voila*, a beautiful and extremely large pond. A brugmansia bush blooms profusely with its orange trumpet flowers, a lantern hibiscus offers up the red flowers, and geraniums and date palms are additional garden delights. *Casa de Reinhart.*

Looking in the opposite direction, this garden has clusters of oyamel, datura, coco plumosa, Mexican sage, and bombax, along with several others. *Casa de Reinhart.*

Looking into the same garden from the rooftop, you see the jungle landscaping with giant bird of paradise, queen palm, yucca, primrose jasmine, and loquat. It absolutely thrives in the climate of San Miguel. *Casa de Reinhart.*

Opposite page:
The opposing angle of the same garden shows pots of daisies encircling the fountain and a blooming jade plant, with its pink flowers, which is a rare sight. *Casa de Reinhart.*

Right:
Avid gardeners need a potting shed and this one is constructed with left-over tile from the home's remodeling job. This has to be the prettiest shed in San Miguel where a lantana bush is beginning to claim the territory. *Casa de Reinhart.*

Plastered and tiled built-in plant troughs line the walkway with euphorbias, jades, and cereus peruvianus. *Casa de la Condessa.*

Left:
The large mesquite tree in the center courtyard grows uninhibited by this home. *Casa de la Condessa.*

Page 168 photo:
Mexican honeysuckle profusely shrouds this fifty-foot iron arbor where electrified punched tin star (*estrella*) lanterns move with the wind and cast beautiful light shadows creating a mystifying ambiance. *Casa Chorro.*

Page 169 photo:
Cascading bougainvillea tumbles over these walls and railings. A pair of ficus trees, geraniums, and ferns occupy most of the courtyard. *Casa Chorro.*

Plastered, low profile walls and flower-filled, built-in planters burst with blooming pansies, petunias, purple lantana, and bougainvillea around this pool. They bring favorite Mexican colors to the backyard area. *Casa de Moser*.

This surrounding garden is a cactus lover's delight. It is absolutely breathtaking, filled with specimens of red hot poker, prickly pear cactus, and a variety of aloes. *La Haciendita*.

Vibrant bougainvillea climbs up a pier on this *portico*. A conglomerate of clay pots and *cantera* animals rests on the stone flooring. *Casa Poco a Poco*.

Agaves, queen palms, aloes, daisies, petunias, and other native plantings follow the curving bricked walkway into this courtyard. *Casa Kino*.

Traditional Mexican style frescoes adorn walls all over desert country. This one, painted by Maja Nostrant for her mother in 1995, carries a love and music theme. Small stone sculptures came from Casas Grandes. *Casa de Franklin*.

Once brightly painted, these now softly muted planter boxes house seasonal flowers. Artist Frank Franklin carved the mesquite wood *hombre* in the foreground in 1983. *Casa de Franklin*.

Towering outside, above the gate, is a huge chinaberry tree. Inside, a Virginia creeper vine is beginning to climb the wall and will provide a beautiful backdrop for the bougainvillea. Indian paintbrush peeks from behind the spineless prickly pear cactus, agave, and agave azul in the foreground. *Casa de Reiner y Gray.*

A tiered brick pedestal and stone carving of the Virgin and Child watch over these gardens where large willowy pampas grass casts a soft shadow on the brick wall. The center brick pathway facilitates work in the herb garden and leads to pomegranate trees and bottlebrush. A massive Virginia creeper vine has almost completely shrouded the facade. *Casa de Reiner y Gray.*

A huge relief sun face smiles on these surroundings where an assortment of pot-filled geraniums ascend the stairway. *Casa del Parque.*

This colorful floral panel of tile (*tablero*), from Delores Hidalgo, hangs over an iron wire garden bench, split leaf philodendrons, and crotons. *Casa de Clark*.

On one side of the lava stone (*laja*) court-yard, this hand-shaped concrete bench is nearly covered in *talavera* tile. In front of it, an old *cantera* wash basin, which was found in a junkyard, was cleverly transformed into a useful plant stand. *Casa de la Cuesta.*

Another level of the same garden has Arizona cypress trees, cassias, salvias, and yuccas. *La Casa que Abraza el Cielo.*

Before any arms form on a saguaro cactus, it has to be fifty to seventy-five years old. This specimen is in good company among Texas rangers, purple plum trees, geraniums, and pansies. *La Casa que Abraza el Cielo.*

Lushly planted flower beds create a desert oasis with variegated agave Americana, sago palms, saguaros, and purple plum trees. *La Casa que Abraza el Cielo.*

Mexican folk art and potted plants decorate this large, split-level courtyard. The outdoor living room (*sala*), covered by a Mission tile roof, is on the third level. An old mesquite tree stands in the center, surrounded by geraniums, yuccas, and dioons. *La Casa Lomita Linda.*

Mesquite wood chairs offer resting places in the courtyard. *La Casa Lomita Linda.*

Beyond the pool gate, flowering pyracantha clings to a ramada. In the foreground, desert petunias, asparagus ferns, rosemary, and geraniums line the brick flooring. *El Castillo.*

This old wooden cart no longer hauls loads, but it still serves a purpose filled with potted geraniums. *La Flor del Desierto*.

Blue agave, golden barrel cactus, saguaros, yucca, and ocotillo are some of the staples in desert gardens. *Red Thunder Ranch*.

After a summer rain, the Texas rangers bloom profusely and become laden with lavender flowers which are irresistible to bees. *Red Thunder Ranch*.

This front yard is enclosed by a brick wall to deter the wildlife, including deer, cattle, and javelinas. While these animals do not bother the saguaros, ocotillo, and mesquites, they might decide to dine on the Texas rangers, prickly pear, and cassias. *Red Thunder Ranch*.

Built-in plastered planter boxes hold a variety of cactus beneath the *citarilla*. *Casa de Alegret*.

A large mesquite tree, planted in a raised bed with ferns, pansies, and verbena, provides sculptural interest along the brick pathway. *Casa de Alegret*.

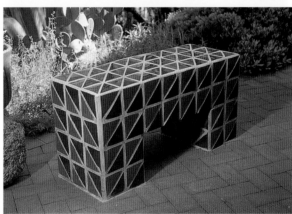

If you have a particular color scheme in mind and can not find a *medio-pañuelo* tile in the two colors you want, there is an alternative solution. This delightful garden bench has two solid color tiles, cobalt blue and terracotta. The square tiles were each cut at a forty-five-degree angle and installed in the eclipsing squares pattern. Notice that when using this method to construct the pattern, there will be a grout line in the forty-five-degree angle. *Casa de Alegret*.

The pathway and beds continue the other direction, showcasing asparagus ferns, aloes in pots, and a creeping fig on the wall. *Casa de Alegret*

The arched and divided-lights style door was salvaged, in pieces, from another house and lovingly restored. Strategically placed fiery bougainvillea, geraniums, gardenias, and desert petunias, along with the Texas ebony tree, create a beautiful sight from both sides of the doorway. *Casa de Alegret*.

Potted bougainvilleas and lavish cactus gardens flank this flagstone walkway, beckoning closer inspection. *Casa de Black*.

Pots of vastly different sizes, shapes, and colors line a patio wall along with geraniums and pencil cactus. *Casa de Black*.

Tulips are short-lived in the desert climate, but here they were blooming beautifully as we tiptoed by in the Springtime. *Casa de Black*.

Both Pages:
This magnificent desert cactus garden is filled with pony tail palms, ocotillos, cereus monstrosus, Mexican fan palms, yuccas, prickly pears, organ pipe cactus, golden barrels, old man cactus, queen palms, and totem pole cactus. *Casa de Black*.

Appendix 1.
Tile Illustration- *Medio-pañuelo*

Medio-pañuelo *Talavera* Tile

 Medio-pañuelo means half-handkerchief. In this instance, we refer to a *talavera* tile with an imaginary line at a 45° angle, with a contrasting color or design on each half of the angle. It offers several different installation methods as evidenced throughout the *casas* in both books.

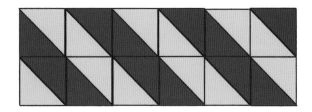 **Angled Stripe**

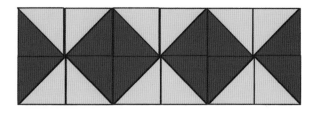 **Diamond**

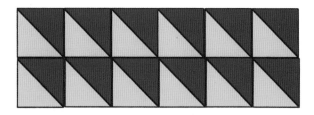 **Eclipsing Squares**

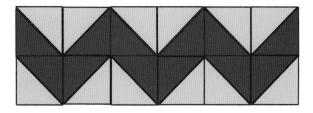 **Herringbone**

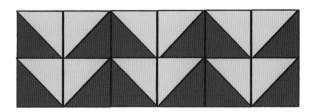 **Sawtooth**

Appendix 2.
Paint Samples

The following paint sample cards were graciously supplied by Dunn-Edwards® Paints and are registered trademarks of Dunn-Edwards Corporation.

Mayan
Fawn
Ocotilla
And the Terracotta colored sample with the following one-gallon formula: 4-3Y36, 8-3Y, 14-2Y 28.8

Fawn

Mayan

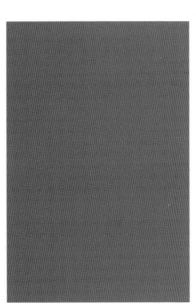

Ocotilla

Terracotta

Glossary

Agua. Water
Alacena. A cupboard in the wall
A la derecha. To the right
Alberca. Pool
Amigo. Friend
Arboles de la vida. Trees of life
Arcada. Arcade or row of arches
Arista. Salient angle
Armario. Cabinet
Arquitecto. Architect
Artes. Arts
Asador. Barbeque grill
Azul. Blue
Azulejo. Glazed tile
Balaustrada. Balustrade
Banco. Bench
Bandidos. Bandits
Baño. Bathroom
Barandales. Underpieces of a balustrade
Barras. Bars or rods
Batea. Painted tray
Baúl. Trunk
Bienvenido. Welcome
Bóveda. Arch or vault
Brasero. Cooking center, usually of masonry with gas or charcoal
Canales. Gutters projecting from roof
Canción. Song
Cantera. Quarry stone
Cantina. Bar
Cariño. Love or affection
Cartas. Letters
Casa. House
Cascada. Waterfall
Casita. Small house

Catrina. Female skeleton
Changuito. Small monkey
Chimenea. Fireplace
Citarilla. Open fence or balustrade usually built of brick or tile
Clavo. Nail or iron spike
Cobalto. Cobalt
Cochera. Garage
Cocina. Kitchen
Columna. Column
Comedor. Dining room
Concha. Shell
Cornisa. Cornice
Corona. Crown (also the name of a Mexican brand of beer)
Corredor. Corridor
Costumbrista. A type of art being produced in Michoacán
Cristo. Chirst, image of Christ crucified
Cúpula. Cupola
Cuña. A light weight brick used for bóveda ceilings
Danos el pan nuestro de cada día. Give us our daily bread
Desayunador. Breakfast room
Elegante. Elegant
Entrada. Entry
Equipale. Pigskin furniture
Escalera. Stairway
Espadaña. Section of a wall crowning the facade with arched openings
Estrella. Star
Exvoto. Painting offering thanks
Fachada exterior. Front facade
Fachada frontal. Front facade
Fachada posterior. Rear facade

Flores. Flowers
Fuente. Fountain
Herradura. Horseshoe shape
Hierro. Iron
Hombre. Man
Huéspedes. Guests
Iglesia. Church
Iluminación. Lighting
Jardín. Garden
Jarrones. Large jars
Laja. A thin flat stone, lava rock
Llamador. Door knocker
Luna. Moon
Maceta. Flowerpot
Maestro. Master craftsman
Mariachi. Mexican street band
Máscara. Mask
Medio-pañuelo. Half-handkerchief pattern
Ménsula. Bracket
Moldura de arco. Arch trim or molding
Mostaza. Mustard
Música. Music
Nicho. Niche
Ojival. A type of arch used in Moorish designs
Ojo de buey. Ox eye
Padre. Father
Pajarito. Little bird
Pecho de paloma. Breast of dove
Perro. Dog
Pescado. Fish
Petatillo. A type of thin brick used for pathways and roofs
Pilar(es). Pillar(s)
Portal(es). Porch(s)
Pórtico. Covered porch, usually at the entry

Postigo. Small door usually inside another door
Portón. Gate
Principal. Main
Puerta. Door
Recámara. Bedroom
Reja. Iron grating or railing, usually in front of a door or window
Repisa. Hanging open shelf
Retablo. Religious painting
Rosa. Pink
Sala. Living room
San. Contraction for Saint
Santo. Saint
Sapo. Frog
Silla. Chair
Sillón. Couch
Sirena. Mermaid
Sol. Sun
Tablero. Panel of tiles, usually comprising a mural
Talavera. Hand-painted, twice-fired, tin-glazed earthenware
Taller. Workshop
Techo. Ceiling
Teja. Clay roof tile
Tipos Mexicanos. Mexican types
Torre. Tower or turret
Tortuga. Turtle
Trastero. Open cupboard
Tristeza. Sadness
Vestíbulo. Vestibule
Viga. Beam
Y. And
Zaguán. Passageway from street to inner courtyard
Zoclo. Baseboard

Bibliography

Garrison, G. Richard and George W. Rustay. *Mexican Houses: A Book of Photographs & Measured Drawings:* New York: Architectural Book Publishing Co., Inc., 1930.

Grizzard, Mary. *Spanish Colonial Art and Architecture of Mexico and the U.S. Southwest.* Lanham: University Press of America, Inc., 1986.

Newcomb, Rexford. *The Spanish House for America: Its Design, Furnishing, and Garden.* Philadelphia: J. B. Lippincott Company, 1927.

O'Gorman, Patricia W. *Patios and Gardens of Mexico.* Stamford: Architectural Book Publishing Co., Inc., 1979.

El patio de mi casa: portadas, portones, zaguanes y patios de la habitación mexicana. Mexico: Instituto del Fondo Nacional de la Vivienda para los Trabajadores, 1990.

Sexton, R.W. *Spanish Influence on American Architecture and Decoration.* New York: Brentano's, 1927.

Shipway, Verna Cook and Warren Shipway. *Decorative Design in Mexican Homes.* New York: Architectural Book Publishing Co., Inc., 1966.

—. *Houses of Mexico: Origins and Traditions.* New York: Architectural Book Publishing Co., Inc., 1970.

—. *Mexican Homes of Today.* New York: Architectural Book Publishing Co., Inc., 1964.

—. *The Mexican House: Old & New.* 1960. Reprint, New York: Architectural Book Publishing Co., Inc., 1963.

—. *Mexican Interiors.* 1962. Reprint, Stamford: Architectural Book Publishing Co., Inc., 1988.

Yañez, Enrique. *18 Residencias de Arquitectos Mexicanos: 18 Homes of Mexican Architects:.* Mexico: Ediciones Mexicanas S.A., 1951.